NG6461

NG6461
The Fake Rubens

Euphrosyne Doxiadis

eris

ERIS

ERIS PRESS LLC
265 Riverside Drive
New York, NY 10025

Cover: detail from edited photograph of NG6461

Distributed by Columbia University Press:
New York, NY, and London, England

Designed by Alex Stavrakas

ISBN 978-1916809-89-5 (paperback)
ISBN 978-1916809-36-9 (hard cover)

eris.press

Contents

NG6461

Author's Notice

Naming creates meaning and produces history. By giving something a name, we come to possess at least part of it, and change the way others refer to and see it. For the sake of clarity, and since this book vigorously asserts that the painting hanging at London's National Gallery is not Peter Paul Rubens's *Samson and Delilah,* references to this work will use the National Gallery's archival designation of this item as NG6461. All other mentions of Rubens's lost masterpiece will be by its original title.

FOR EMMA AND NIKIFOROS, WHO LOVE THE TRUTH

Seeds of Doubt

Glory to that Homer of painting, the father of warmth and enthusiasm in the art where he puts all others in the shade, not, perhaps, because of his perfection in any one direction, but because of that hidden force—that life and spirit—which he put into everything he did.

— Eugène Delacroix[1]

It was in Madrid, at the age of twenty-one, that I fell in love with Peter Paul Rubens. We had missed each other by many centuries—his last visit to Spain ended in 1629—but he still waited for me in the basement galleries of the Prado. The museum in those days was austere—almost Spartan. It hadn't been renovated, and its facilities compared unfavourably with its counterparts in Italy or France. The sobriety of the building made a suitable home, I thought, for much of the art inside: the pitiless honesty of Diego Velázquez's royal portraits; the Pinturas Negras of Goya's last, tormented years, as well as his prints of the Disasters of War; and the mystical paintings of Doménikos Theotokópoulos—El Greco—the foreigner in Spain. In the basement, I stumbled with astonishment into the world of Rubens, his panels covering wall after wall in room after room with an explosion of colour. I wandered through the corridors, delighted by what I was seeing. A man of sunshine and of spirituality lay behind these paintings, and I will forever remember the impression he made on me that day.

I stopped in front of *The Birth of the Milky Way*. It hadn't been cleaned—nor had most of Rubens's works—but it was still stunning. My friend Iñigo, a draughtsman, considered it in silence for a few minutes and then remarked, "Isn't this the visual equivalent of Beethoven's 'Ode to Joy'?" I agreed; I was in love.

Eager to know more, I read a pamphlet about Rubens's visits to Madrid in 1603 and 1628. He went there the first time as an artist in the service of Vincenzo I Gonzaga, Duke of Mantua; the second time as a diplomat, sent to discuss with Philip IV of Spain terms for peace between England and Spain. Rubens was known to the Duke of Buckingham—a close friend of King Charles I—who was negotiating to buy Rubens's collection of antiquities. Rubens had pleaded with the Duke that England should not side with the Dutch against the Spanish rule of Flanders and, despite King Philip's initial apprehensions about a painter being involved in diplomacy, he was summoned to Madrid in August 1628. After seven months, he would continue on to England where he would obtain both a treaty of peace for the two countries, and a knighthood for himself.

Despite the pressures of his diplomatic undertakings, Rubens's creative fervour never waned. "I am painting here, as I do wherever I find myself", he wrote to his friend Pierre Dupuy on 2 December 1628.[2] During his stay in Madrid, Rubens painted portraits of every member of the royal family. "It seems incredible that in so short a time, and in the midst of so many duties, he could have painted so many pictures", marvelled Francisco Pacheco in his illuminating chronicle of Rubens's sojourn in Spain.[3] Pacheco's primary source of information was probably his son-in-law, who was none other than King Philip's gifted young court painter, Diego Velázquez. Pacheco even indulged in a bit of fatherly flattery on Velázquez's account: "Rubens praised Velázquez's works very highly because of his modesty. They visited the Escorial together"[4]. Sadly, this is all we have from that meeting between these two giants of European painting.

A PAINTER'S PAINTER

Standing in front of his works in the Prado, I could understand why, for so many artists, Rubens has been a painter's painter. His distinguished contemporaries clamoured to collaborate with him, and he went on to inspire countless generations of artists since: Watteau, Delacroix, and Cézanne were all in awe of this colourist *par excellence*, whose palette had the clarity of van Eyck, the richness of Titian, and the drunken *joie de vivre* of the Impressionists. His women glow from within, their skin radiant like translucent porcelain. The sapphire and saffron cloaks of his painted men billow in the wind like liquid jewels. You can all but hear the ruby and emerald taffeta dresses of his ladies rustling up marble stairs, his soft-hued choruses mingling with the fading evening skies. His brushstrokes dance across the smooth surface of the seasoned oak panels that were lovingly crafted for him by the master panel-makers of his native Antwerp. Luxury, calm, and voluptuousness had everything to do with painting as Peter Paul Rubens practised it. He was gifted with both a rare artistry and a brilliant mind, "mixing his colours with his brains" in Turner's words.

As an aspiring artist, I was impressed as much with Rubens's attitude as with his skill. And, although my passion for Rubens was born in the Prado, it was Cézanne who had first introduced me to him. As an art student at the Slade in London in the 1960s, I had an obsession with Cézanne. Learning that Rubens was Cézanne's favourite painter, I began to look at him in a different light, sitting for entire afternoons in front of his works in the National Gallery.

During my years at the Slade, I would spend all my spare time in museums and galleries, studying and drawing from their collections. All first-year students of painting were required to copy a picture by a great master. I chose *Man with a Pipe*, a portrait of Cézanne's gardener that was hanging in the Courtauld Institute. In those days, the Courtauld galleries were located in a lovely building on Woburn Square. It was like entering someone's private apartment to admire their art collection. Every day, for about a month, I was left alone in that small, intimate space with a roomful of Impressionist painters. It was a magical experience.

On one such day, as I was walking around with my painting, I bumped into the Head of the Slade. "Where are you making off to with that Cézanne?" He asked cheekily. "May I see it?" Of course he was just being kind, but for me this was the first glimpse into the issues involved in the reproduction of paintings. My copy of Cézanne was actually fractionally smaller than the original. But that is customary: all museum copies *must* be slightly different in size from the original to allay the danger of forgery. If you alter the scale, a painting will always look slightly off. The National Gallery was especially wary of the threat of fakes. In a similar incident that happened there, I was about halfway through a copy of Jan Vermeer's *A Young Woman Seated at the Virginals*, when the Gallery authorities stopped me. They asked me to start again, this time using a smaller canvas: mine was too close in size to the original. As a naïve nineteen-year-old, I had no notion of copies as potential forgeries. I certainly never thought I could reproduce a painting so well that it might be confused with the original.

     SEEDS OF DOUBT

Like other architects, my father loved Cézanne, so I gave him my copy of *Man with a Pipe*. When he passed away in 1975, my mother gave the painting back to me, and I decided to put it into a very expensive frame to create the illusion that it was authentic, thus serving as a decoy for burglars. I hoped they would take this copy, rather than other, much-loved paintings that had been given to me by fellow artists. Fortunately, no art-loving burglar ever paid me a visit, so I still have this old student copy of *Man with A Pipe*.

NG6461

The saga which was to take up so much of my life started in 1984, when I visited the National Gallery after several years' absence from London. Walking along a wide passageway, I remember seeing a gaudy picture that looked like the Rubens idiom, but extremely badly executed. It was so unconvincing that it didn't even look like a museum copy. The execution was awkward, the draughtsmanship clumsy, the colours garish, and the depiction of textures weak. It reminded me of those bad copies that are sold to tourists on the Bayswater Road [1].

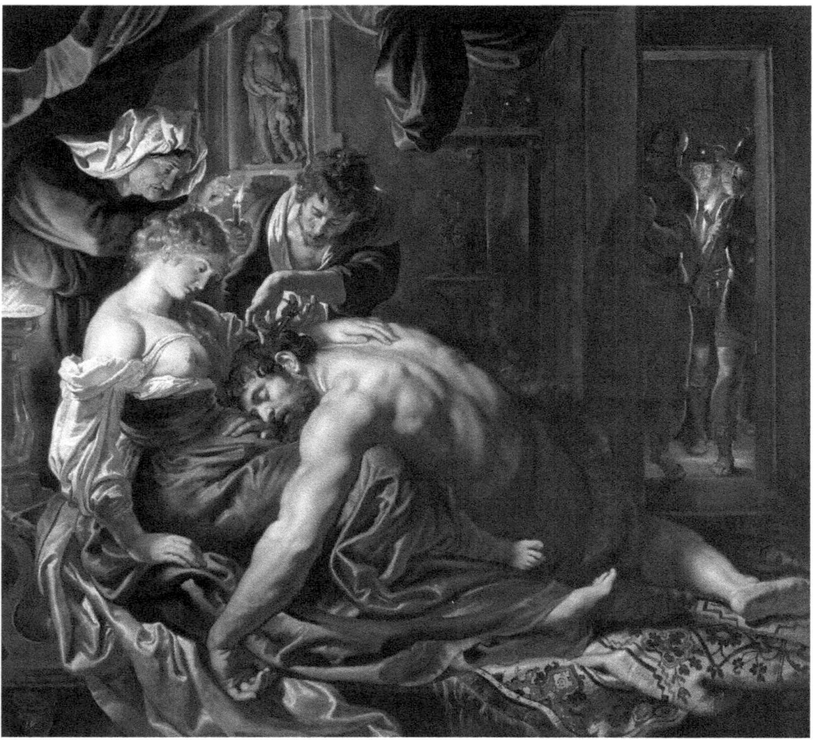

1. NG6461: The contested painting that hangs in London's National Gallery.

I read the label: *"Samson and Delilah* by Peter Paul Rubens". It was a depiction of the Old Testament story of the Israelite hero Samson who was betrayed by the beautiful Delilah, to whom he had confided that the secret of his superhuman strength lay in his hair. In this famous episode from *The Book of Judges,* the fickle woman, in the pay of the Philistines, has Samson lay his head on her lap. As he sleeps, she calls in a servant to cut off his locks, rendering him helpless before his enemies. This was a popular subject in the strict Catholic society of seventeenth-century Flanders, intended as a cautionary tale on the evils of succumbing to lust. It also provided artists with a convenient pretext to depict sensual female beauty without censure.[5]

'BLINK MOMENT', 1984

The first time that I saw NG6461, I felt a sudden jolt. I was immediately certain that this painting was not one painted by Rubens. It was my Malcolm Gladwell 'blink moment'[6]—the moment I saw the thing for what it really was: a bad imitation.

What was hanging in front of me was a broken-up image, a technicolor patchwork. That first impression was enough. This may sound arrogant, but many art historians have written on the critical importance of the first impression. A great picture grabs one the moment one first lays eyes on it. An inferior one, having been calculated in execution, leaves the viewer unmoved. "Correct attributions generally appear spontaneously and 'prima vista'", wrote the German art historian Max Friedländer.[7] A great painting has an inherent magnetism; it is imposing and demands attention.

When I stood in front of NG6461 in the Gallery, the painting looked glossy and brash beside the works of Rubens that surrounded it. I stepped closer. The film of paint looked as if it was gripping the fibres of a linen cloth **[2]**, instead of sitting flatly on

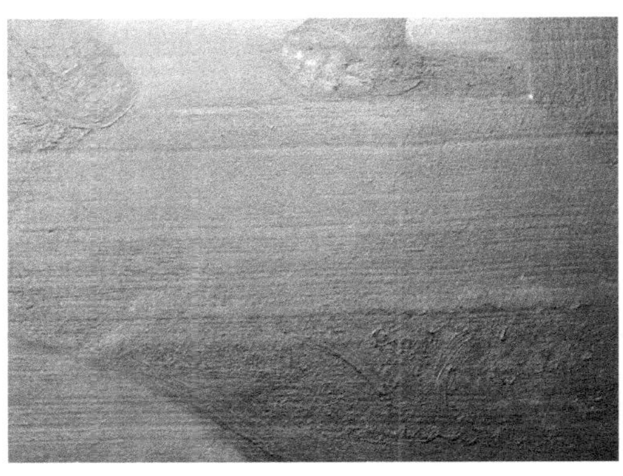

2. NG6461 (detail): Brushstrokes on what appears to be linen canvas.

     SEEDS OF DOUBT

the smooth finish of a primed oak panel. The flowing, twisting brushstrokes that are so characteristic of Rubens were nowhere to be seen. Instead, the brushstrokes appeared uncertain and non-dynamic [3, 4] and, as a result, the forms lacked definition.

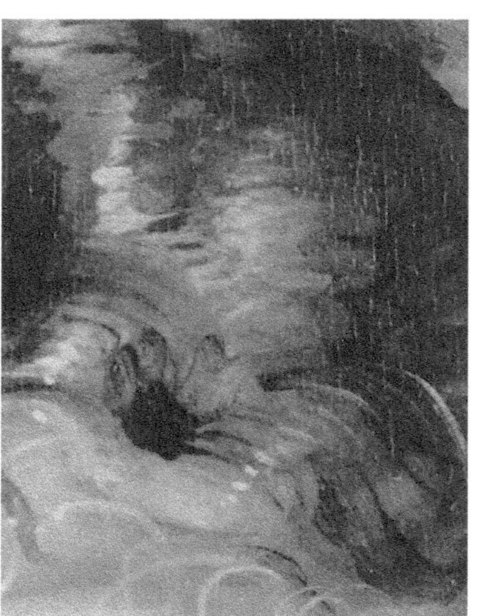
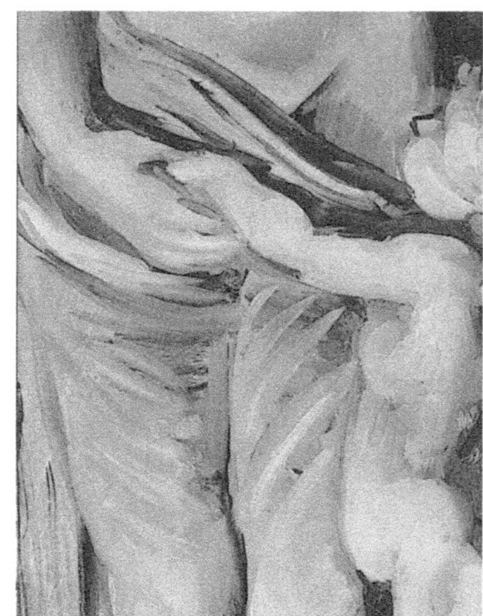

3, 4. NG6461 (detail): Sloppy and hurried style, uncharacteristic of a master painter like Rubens.

The pigments had been applied sparingly, in a patchy way—a technique that Rubens used mostly in his *modelli* (preparatory oil sketches), and certainly not before 1620 in his large paintings, where tightly woven brushstrokes cover entire forms. In several places, the underpainting showed through like bald patches. The composition looked disjointed and oddly unstructured. Most striking of all, Samson's toes were chopped off by the edge of the painting, making the whole thing like a detail of a classical pyramidal composition.

I saw no point at the time in investigating this further, so I just went on my way without giving the painting a second thought. In 1987, I decided to return to art school. I enrolled for an honours course in Painting at Wimbledon School of Art, where I became friends with Steve Harvey, a painter who reminded me of Egon Schiele. Steve had just suffered a breakup with a fellow student of ours, and to cheer him up him I suggested we go to the National Gallery, which had always been my cure for everything. We took the train to Charing Cross, threaded our way through the pigeons and tourists of Trafalgar Square, and entered the domed lobby of the National Gallery. It was to be a portentous visit—it would affect the next thirty-six years of my life, and shatter any illusions I harboured about the art world.

"Let's start with my favourite painter, Rubens", I suggested. We began with the *Minerva Protects Pax from Mars ('Peace and War')*, the masterpiece he had produced in England in 1629–30, inspired by his diplomatic success, and presented to King Charles I. We looked at oil sketches, landscapes, and portraits. Being a very talented painter himself, Steve was soon able to see what I was so excited about. "Even the depiction of the bust of Hippocrates is handled like the depiction of a live human being", he noted, as we studied an astonishing portrait of one of Rubens's friends: *Portrait of Ludovicus Nonnius*. Rubens endowed the statues he painted with the same animated vitality, the same *vis poetica*, as everything else he painted. Then I told Steve I'd show him an awful "Rubens" I'd seen some years earlier. We went and stood in front of NG6461.

TWO PAINTERS EXAMINE THE PICTURE

Before us, the hulking figure of Samson lay asleep, seemingly exhausted, with his head in Delilah's lap. She leaned back, her shoulder and breasts bare, while still looking down on him. Behind her, a man leans over to snip off a lock of Samson's hair under the watchful gaze of an old woman holding a candle. In the background to the right, five Philistine soldiers are huddled in the doorway, waiting to pounce on their now-helpless prey. A statue of Venus and Cupid in the background reminds us of the seductive power of lust, the cause of Samson's downfall.

According to the label, the *Samson and Delilah* was privately commissioned by Nicolaas Rockox, then Mayor of Antwerp, to hang over the fireplace of his large living room [5]. It was painted

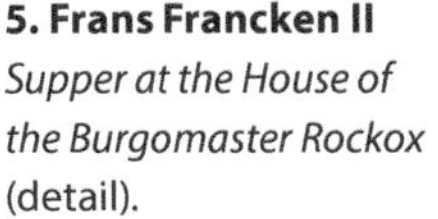

5. Frans Francken II
Supper at the House of the Burgomaster Rockox (detail).

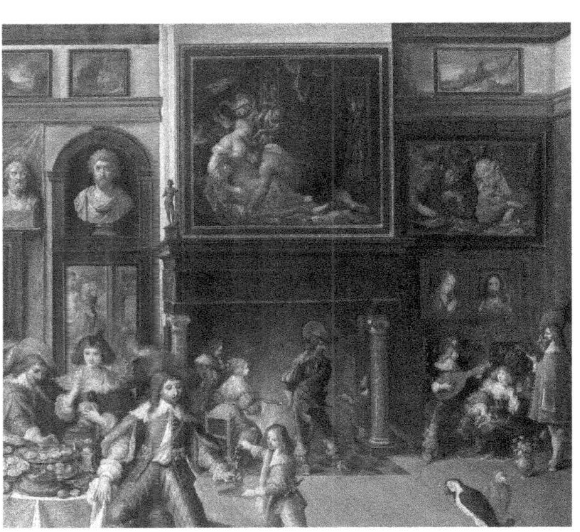

SEEDS OF DOUBT

around 1609, shortly after Rubens returned to Antwerp from Italy, where he had spent eight formative years in the service of the Duke of Mantua.

Just as on the first occasion I'd seen the painting three years earlier, I was struck by the overall crudeness of its style, as well as by the absence of a consistent visual code. The transitions between tones and colours lacked subtlety, and the tonal values were incorrect in relation to the four sources of light: the enormous torch behind Delilah's back, the old crone's candle, a flaming torch held by one of the Philistines and, finally, the candle under the statue of Venus and Cupid. The dull brown background was painted with very sparse brushstrokes, thus allowing the pale underpainting to show through, over-illuminating the scene. The background did not recede enough, jumping, instead, out into the foreground. The shadows created by the candle should have been warm rather than cool; conversely, there was no cool shading in Delilah's face.

All these anomalies would have been acceptable had the painter managed to make them work—after all, we know all too well that a painting is not necessarily a faithful representation of physical reality. But here they simply didn't work. The elusive illusion of reality had not been achieved.

DULL DELILAH

Delilah, who had such power over Samson that he finally told her his vital secret, surely ought to have been depicted as the quintessence of femininity. At the moment of his defeat by her Philistine countrymen, her face should have looked radiantly triumphant, or regretful, or thoughtful—it should have been showing *some* emotion. Instead, this Delilah looks down dully, lustreless in body and spirit, as if half-asleep herself. Rubens's brushes usually tingle with excitement whenever he paints female flesh. Young women in his paintings have a translucent fragility, an effect that he achieved by using a special protein and oil mixture called *thixotrope*. This gives the flesh a lifelike semblance, as well as a luminosity and a glow from within. Interestingly, Willem de Kooning used a similar emulsion (rumoured to be mayonnaise) to give his female nudes the same sensual and glowing effect. Poussin used a comparable technique of placing a transparent colour over a luminous white in order to create the unique ultramarine blues that became his trademark. And Renoir—who emulated Rubens's nudes to great effect—began his artistic career as a painter of porcelain cups and saucers. He would therefore have also been applying paint on a bright, white background like bone-porcelain, on which colours become enhanced by the white shining through. Cézanne's watercolours have the same quality, but in his case the white of the paper replaces the white undercoat used in oil paintings.

Rubens's masterful handling of this technique is characteristic of his personal touch. Delilah's doughy, pink flesh bears no resemblance to the pale, translucent, delicious décolleté of Susanna Lunden, Rubens's young sister-in-law-to-be portrayed in *Portrait of Susanna Lunden*, which was then hanging right next to NG6461. By comparison, Delilah's exposed breasts are like dull dumplings of opaque, pasty plasticine, uniform in colour [6]. The nipples of Rubens's nudes are an appetising cherry pink, whereas Delilah's nipples are bland and have no definition. Where was the sexiness that inspired Samson's lust, the lust that was to be his downfall? Where is Delilah's star quality? Where is her beauty?

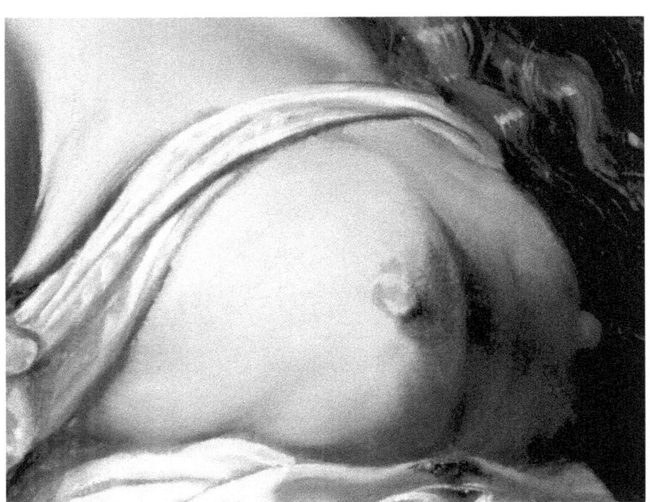

6. NG6461 (detail): Delilah's exposed breasts do not resemble the finessed nude details in other works by Rubens.

CRAQUELURE

I looked more closely at Delilah's skin. In the pallor of Rubens's depictions of women's flesh it is often possible to detect a network of fine cracks, caused by the movement of paint in changing temperatures over the centuries. The conservators working on Rubens's *The Elevation of the Cross* in Antwerp [7, 8]—contemporary with *Samson and Delilah*—commented on "the different conditions of the surface from one plank to the other, differences which appear in the network of the *craquelure*, a result, on the

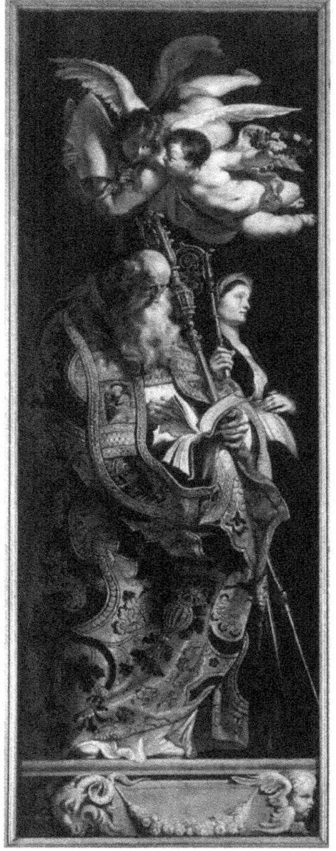
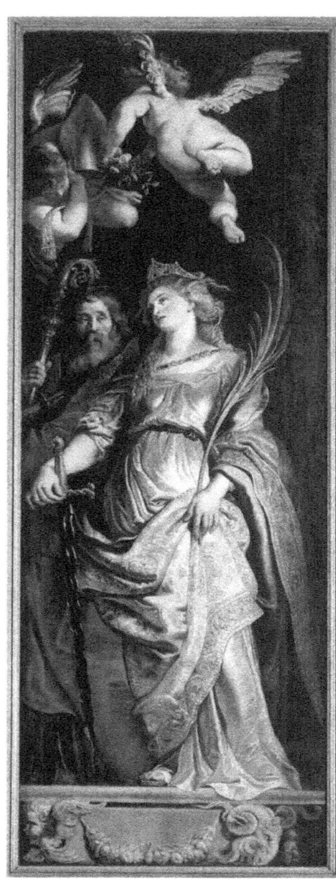

one hand, of the wood's subsequent movements because of variations of humidity and, on the other, of the different thickness of the layers and the interactions between the pigments, the binding media and their nature"[8]. This is especially obvious in the décolleté of Susana Lunden, which is lined with this fine *craquelure* [9]. By comparison, Delilah's flesh [10] displays almost

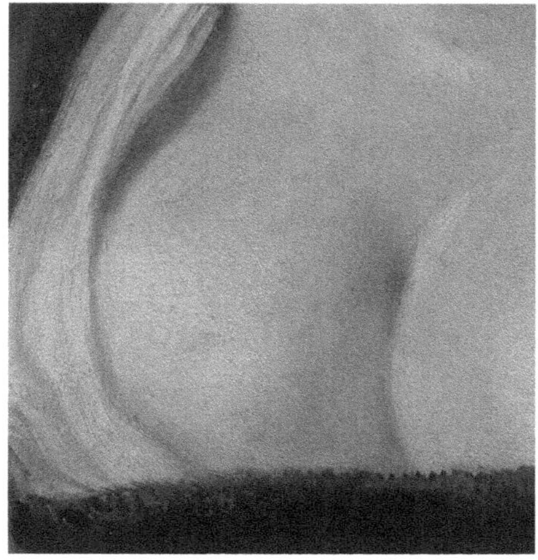
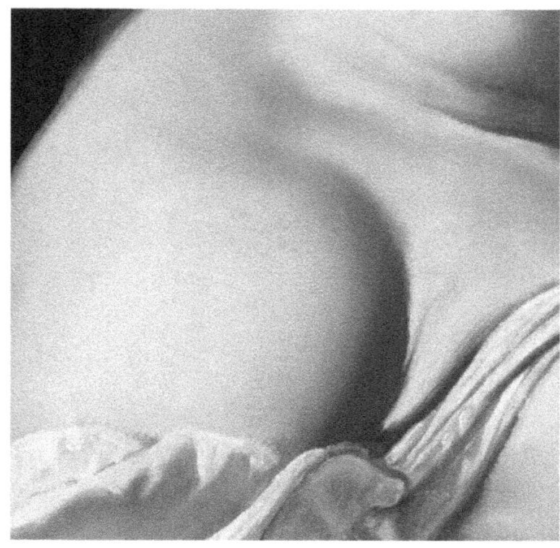

no evidence of this delicate ageing which one would expect to
see in an early seventeenth-century oil painting. Absent, too, was
another 'trademark' feature of Rubens's technique which he frequently used in the depiction of fabrics: the areas of thick white
impasto overlaid with translucent glazes that allowed the under-
lying white to glow from underneath. A brilliant example of this
masterly technique can be seen in the magnificent painting of St
Catherine's dress on the reverse side of the right panel of *The Elevation of the Cross* in Antwerp Cathedral which dates from 1611.

THE CARPET

As Steve and I looked at the painting more closely, we began to
notice even more disconcerting details. The rug is painted in a curiously neo-impressionist way; a tasselled fringe sprouts from its
side—something that would never be the case with an actual rug,
where the loom construction would have fringes only on opposite
ends—and the flower patterns do not follow the undulations of
the material. Things get even more incredible once we consider
the fact—as confirmed to me by a world-renowned rug expert—
that the design emulates that of late seventeenth-century Turkish
rugs from West Anatolia that could simply not have been found by
the artist in Antwerp in 1609 **[11]**.

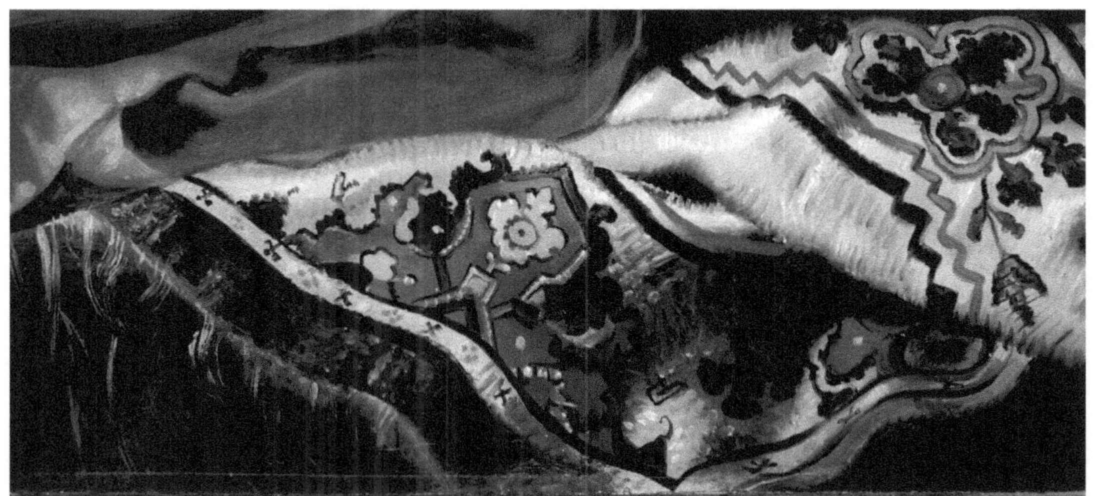

11. NG6461 (detail):
Patterns and decorations
in the rug design that
are inconsistent with the
painting's claimed age.

PROPORTIONS

Proportions and perspectives are incorrect—the old woman
is not close enough to the other figures to illuminate the scene
with her candle; Samson's head rests at an awkward angle on

Delilah's lap; his rippling back is unnaturally wide, and a nondescript area of anatomy lurks between his chunky thighs and the fur rug draped across his legs. A drip of paint stains the surface in the area under Delilah's armpit, an unthinkable gaffe for *any* early-seventeenth-century painter with even the most basic training—let alone the greatest master of technique.

THE TOES

I stepped back to get a better look. Suddenly it hit me: the composition was hopelessly awry. All the figures are squashed up on the left, yet Samson's toes have been carelessly lopped off at the bottom right hand corner of the frame, making the whole picture look like a badly framed detail. I wondered whether the panel had been cut for some reason, but then dismissed this thought: at the

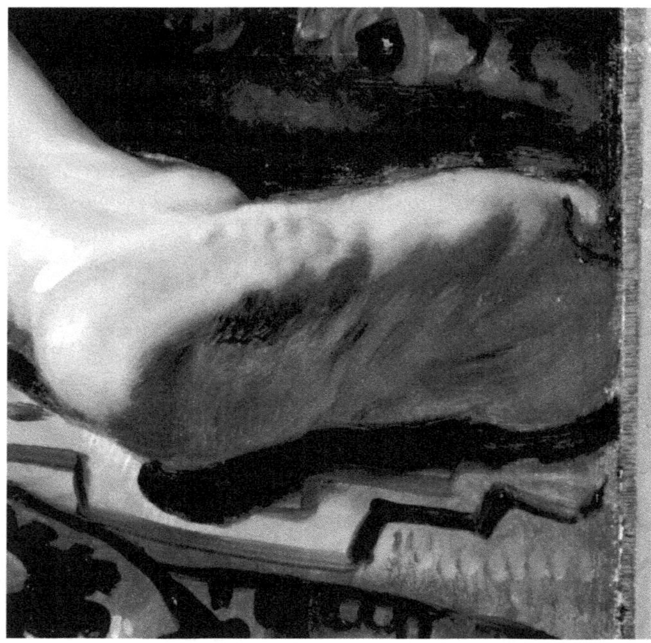

12. NG6461 (detail): Samson's missing toes, an uncommon and bizarre artistic choice to make in 1609.

inner edge of the frame it was possible to see clearly where the paint ended and the bare wood continued **[12]**. Moreover, if the panel had originally been larger, Samson's missing foot would have extended well beyond the doorframe, thus breaking up the pyramidal composition of the figures. Fresh from Italy and filled with a deep knowledge of Michelangelo, Titian, Veronese, and Caravaggio, Rubens would never have forgiven himself such a clumsy structure.[9] Instead, he would have included Samson's toes

in their entirety, which—as well as endowing the hero with all
the dynamics of his strength—would also compositionally make
sense, since the classical pyramid of the figures would then have
been complete. Steve was as horrified by NG6461 as I. Neither of
us knew that it had been bought by the National Gallery seven
years earlier, in 1980, for £2.5 million!

THE BANQUETING HOUSE

In the space of a single afternoon, Steve had been convinced: he
was as stunned by Rubens as I had been in the Prado. But there
was one more thing I wanted to show him. We emerged from the
hush of the Gallery into the busy square outside, and set off in the
direction of the Houses of Parliament, sidestepping tourists and
government officials. Big Ben chimed in the distance.

There were no crowds queueing for the Banqueting House. Designed for King James I by the seventeenth-century architect Ini-
go Jones and built in 1622, this vast hall is still occasionally used
for royal receptions and state functions. It was the only wing of
the Royal Palace of Whitehall to survive a devastating fire in
1698, although the structure itself had replaced an earlier one
burnt down in 1619.

After the gift of *Minerva Protects Pax from Mars ('Peace and
War')*, King Charles I rewarded Rubens with a lucrative contract
(a princely sum of £3,000) to decorate the ceiling of the Banqueting
Hall with nine magnificent canvasses collectively titled after the
main work: *The Apotheosis of James I*. The curators have thought-
fully equipped the hall with two large mirrored tables on wheels,
so visitors can admire the paintings reflected in their surfaces
rather than craning their necks to squint at the ceiling.

The commission took several years to complete, and Rubens
was not paid for another three. On 30 January 1649, King Charles
stepped out of a first-floor window on the north side of the Banqueting Hall onto the scaffold where he was beheaded.

SIÂN

Steve went back to Wimbledon and told our studio mate, Siân
Hopkinson (also a figurative painter), all about the fake Rubens
in the National Gallery. Like Steve, Siân was a natural-born
painter with a sharp eye. The next day she went back with him
to have a look. Siân loved Rubens but was horrified by NG6461.
She remembered reading that the National Gallery had bought

the painting at Christie's in 1980 for £2.53 million. At the time, it had been the second highest sum ever paid on a painting, so it had caused quite a stir. Many people were scandalised that the National Gallery had spent so much taxpayer's money for it.

Siân began plaguing me in the corridors of Wimbledon School of Art. "We have to do something about this fake Rubens", she would say every time we would cross paths, fixing me with her grey-blue eyes. Porcelain-pale with long, dark hair, Siân had a quiet intensity that I found compelling. But between my family life and my schoolwork, I had very little time for research. In all honesty, I felt paralysed by the magnitude of my discovery, and of the consequences it might have. In spite of my unresponsiveness, Siân kept insisting that we should pursue the matter.

Finally, one day, I gave in.

"OK", I sighed. "Let's do it".

It was a decision I would live to regret.

Rubens in Antwerp:
Rockox's Painting in Context

Rubens, river of oblivion, garden of indolence,
Pillow of cool flesh where one cannot love,
But where life moves and whirls incessantly
Like the air in the sky and the tide in the sea.

— Charles Baudelaire[1]

Siân, Steve, and I had been reading about Rubens's years in Antwerp, and had compiled an impressive patchwork of stories of war, peace, and art. To see the (real) *Samson and Delilah* in its artistic context, it is important to look back over the eight years that the young Rubens had spent in Italy, where he saw, and was influenced by, the work of the great artists of the Renaissance, and also that of his contemporaries.

Already an independent painter trained in Antwerp, in May 1600, twenty-two-year-old Rubens travelled on horseback to Venice, where he discovered the works of Titian, Veronese, and Tintoretto. From Venice he went on to Mantua, where he became court painter to the Duke of Mantua, Vincenzo I Gonzaga. Another painter at the court was the portraitist Frans Pourbus, while Monteverdi was the court musician. There Rubens studied the work of his predecessor at the Mantuan court, Raphael's pupil Giulio Romano, and he reworked drawings by Romano and his assistant Francesco Primaticcio. He also admired the great Andrea Mantegna.

When, in 1601–2, he went to Rome to make copies for the Duke of Mantua, Rubens became familiar with the paintings of Michelangelo and Raphael (of whose works in the Sistine Chapel and the Vatican Stanze he made copies), as well as Leonardo da Vinci, Correggio, and Andrea del Sarto. He further explored Renaissance art through his study and retouching of other artists' drawings, and himself made drawings after antique sculptures. He was also highly impressed and influenced by his contemporaries Caravaggio (of whose *The Entombment of Christ* painting he later made a copy) and the German landscape painter Adam Elsheimer, who became a close friend.

In 1603–4, Rubens was sent to Spain on a mission for the Duke of Mantua, and wrote enthusiastically to the Duke about many splendid works of Titian, of Raphael, and others[2] in the royal collections. In Italy he received many commissions for pictures. Finally, in October 1608, news that his mother was seriously ill drew him back to Antwerp, which he reached in December, sadly just after her death.

In January 1609, Peter Paul's beloved brother Philip became town clerk in Antwerp, while Nicolaas Rockox was Burgomaster (Mayor). The two men's friendship became such that in 1611 Rockox became godfather to Philip's son—less than a month before Philip's sudden death. Just as his brother must have owed his appointment as town clerk to Rockox, so Peter Paul probably owed his first large commission after his return from Italy—*Adoration of the Magi* (painted *c.*1609–10 for the Antwerp Town Hall; now in the Prado, Madrid)—to the mayor.

Rubens had arrived at a blessed moment for the city: on 9 April 1609 the Twelve Years' Truce was signed, bringing about a ceasefire between the Dutch Republic and Spain. One day later, Rubens would write: "during this period it is believed that our country will flourish again"[3]. In the same year, he accepted the prestigious position of court painter to the Regents of the Netherlands, the Archduke Albert, and the Infanta Isabella. Their court was in Brussels but, exceptionally, Rubens was permitted to remain in Antwerp, where he lived with his wife Isabella Brandt. Paintings of this period include his marriage portrait, *Honeysuckle Bower*. Soon he was asked to paint altarpieces for Antwerp, Ghent, Brussels, and Mechelen.

To handle the increasing volume of new commissions, Rubens had to set up a large studio. There he painted important works and gradually built up a workshop where he employed assistant pupils for secondary tasks. There have been several misunderstandings about the role of Rubens's assistants, most of which can surely be traced to an account given by Otto Sperling, a physician to the Danish Court who attended Rubens's studio in

1621 (twelve years after *Samson and Delilah* was completed).
Here is what he said:

> A good number of young painters [were] each occupied on a differ-
> ent work, for which Mr Rubens had provided chalk drawings with
> touches of colour added here and there. The young men had to work
> these up fully in paint, until finally Mr Rubens would add the last
> touches with the brush and colours. All this is considered as Rubens's
> work; thus he has gained a large fortune, and kings and princes have
> heaped gifts and jewels upon him.[4]

Sperling's conclusion is cynical: Rubens is portrayed as running
a production line, passing everything off as autograph. But Sperling was in Rubens's studio for only a few minutes, as a foreign
visitor; and he wrote up the account in 1673, a good fifty years
after his visit.

That Sperling was wrong in his description is evident from
Rubens's enormous correspondence, where the artist goes out of
his way to make a clear distinction between different categories of
paintings. For example, he would charge much more for what he
described as "original, entirely by my hand", as opposed to works
that were classified in descending order according to the extent of
his personal involvement, ending with copies made entirely by his
pupils, which were the cheapest.[5]

On the other hand, Sperling's text provides us with a rare in-
sight into the method Rubens used to transfer the designs of his
paintings from small-size oil sketches, his *modelli*, to full-scale
works. We learn that he drew the entire design with chalk on the
prepared wooden panel or canvas; then he painted small daubs of
colour in each shape as a sample to indicate which colour he—or
the assigned assistant—would fill in at a later stage. The theory
that assistants transferred designs from Rubens's *modelli* to the
large-scale panels, which has sadly become widely accepted, is, in
my opinion, entirely unsubstantiated[6]. This theory simply doesn't
make sense, since the *modelli* are different from the corresponding
large paintings in design: Rubens's style is too free and flowing to
have been mechanically copied from small to large.

But let us go back to Antwerp in the years immediately follow-
ing Rubens's return from Italy. His first major altarpiece was *The
Elevation of the Cross*, which was ordered in 1610 by the church of
St Walburga in Antwerp. A large triptych on oak panel, it was

moved in the early nineteenth century to Antwerp Cathedral, where it balances his second important altarpiece, *The Descent from the Cross*, which was commissioned in 1611 for the altar of the Guild of Arquebusiers. The president of that guild was Nicolaas Rockox, and he was responsible for the commission of *The Descent from the Cross*, as he was to be (directly or indirectly) behind many of the artist's commissions. Rockox was very eager to see Antwerp restored to its former glory. Being a deeply religious man, a humanist, and a learned connoisseur, he would have entertained a large circle of friends and important figures in the parlour dominated by *Samson and Delilah*. He and his wife had no children, and it was to Rubens that he turned when he planned their tomb—a relatively small triptych in the Recollects Convent in Antwerp.

Rubens referred to Rockox as "my friend and patron"[7], calling him "an honest man and a connoisseur of antiquities, a good administrator, and all in all a gentleman of the most blameless reputation"[8]. Several important conclusions can be drawn from Rubens's close friendship with Rockox and from the importance that the latter had for the artist as his patron. It is inconceivable that Rubens would have used studio assistance for a work intended as a *tour de force* to advertise his remarkable skills just after his return from Italy. The picture would surely have belonged among those that he proudly classified as "original, entirely by my hand". While the *Samson and Delilah* was intended for a domestic setting, there is no reason why such matters of personal 'handwriting' as is the form of the brushstrokes and the process of working on lightly-toned *imprimatura* should differ from contemporaneous Rubens works such as *The Elevation of the Cross* and *The Descent from the Cross*.

Opening Pandora's Box

I resolved to find out how the painting had ended up in the National Gallery's collection. There had been quite a furore in the press following the acquisition, so I began looking for newspaper reports. On 12 July, 1980, the day after the sale, Geraldine Norman, the Sale Room Correspondent for *The Times*, wrote:

> Christie's hammer fell at £2.3 million; the main competitor was in an anteroom, his bids being relayed to the main saleroom by telephone. The auctioneers would give no indication of his identity yesterday. On top of the £2.3 million, the Gallery has to pay Christie's the standard buyer's premium of £230,000—'a service charge for which no service is rendered', Sir Geoffrey Agnew termed it yesterday. As head of Agnew's, the Bond Street dealers, he bid for the picture on behalf of the Gallery yesterday. Agnew's will also be charging a 'nominal' fee for advice.[1]

A week later, in another article, this time for *The Spectator*, entitled "The Unkindest Cut", Norman enquired rhetorically:

> Hardly anybody has asked why the National Gallery thought fit to spend £2.3 million of taxpayers' money on a vast Rubens oil painting which, at least in my opinion, is far less attractive than the delightful Rubens portraits and landscapes it already possesses. However, if this is a subject for controversy, it has been overshadowed by the charge of £230,000 which Christie's made to the Gallery for the privilege of acquiring it at one of their auctions. Should have argued that Christie's should have waived their buyers' premium charge for the sake of the nation.[2]

Under the headline "Fury Over Rubens Fee", Judith Judd also raised the contentious issue of the service charge a few weeks after the auction:

> Dealers and museum directors argue this service does not exist. Even the auctioneer's catalogue has to be paid for. In the case of buyers such as the National Gallery, they say the charges seem particularly ludicrous since the gallery does not need the services of Christie's to tell it that *Samson and Delilah* is a Rubens.[3]

The ten-percent premium from the auction [13] (coordinated, incidentally, by Christie's board member Gregory Martin, erstwhile curator at the National Gallery) brought the total cost to the taxpayer to £2,530,000. For that sum, the National Gallery must have been confident they were getting an authentic Rubens. Had the museum's experts not noticed the stylistic blunders that were so howlingly obvious to Siân, Steve, and me?

13. 11 July 1980: NG6461 being auctioned at Christie's.

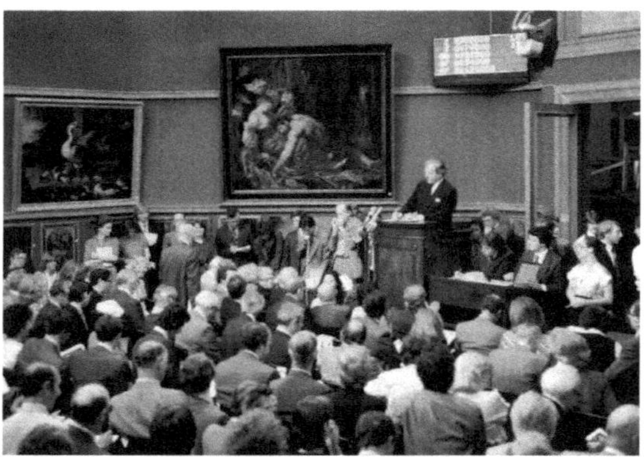

AUCTION HOUSES

I was familiar with the chicanery that is endemic at (especially high-value) auctions, such as shill bidding, the practice of placing bids for the purpose of driving up the hammer price. Conversely, most museums—and, specifically, the National Gallery—observed standard policy that, before a new acquisition was considered (on the recommendation of the Director and a specialist curator), the work in question should be brought in to be examined by the Trustees, who would have to approve a purchase. Could the National Gallery have foreseen that the painting would cost such an astronomical sum? Had the Trustees given Agnew *carte blanche* to secure the painting at any price?

In the hope of finding answers to these questions, I went to the Witt Library. The first thing I found was a poor-quality photocopy of the Christie's auction catalogue, a slim volume dedicated exclusively to *Samson and Delilah* (NG6461). The painting was lot number 134; apparently it had been tagged onto an Old Masters Sale taking place that same morning of 11 July 1980. Significantly, the catalogue contained no price estimate for the painting prior to the sale, but it did include a long-disused title of nobility that Christie's unearthed in a desperate attempt to increase the artist's 'prestige'. But history has freed Rubens from the need for a title.

Given that the National Gallery had blown the greater part of its annual acquisition budget on a single work, I assumed (and hoped) its provenance would be bulletproof. Instead, the provenance as presented in the auction catalogue seemed sketchy at best; it was riddled with prefatory adverbs like "probably" and "perhaps". I noticed that a full page was dedicated to a bibliography—termed 'literature', a standard term of art historical jargon—which looked impressive enough at first glance. The painting had been exhibited in a major Rubens retrospective at the Royal Museum of Fine Arts in Antwerp as recently as 1977, celebrating the four-hundredth anniversary of Rubens's birth—something that implied approval by modern scholarship. The current owners had chosen to remain anonymous: the painting was obliquely referred to by Christie's as "The Property of a Family". The provenance read as follows (italics/emphases mine):

Probably painted for Nicolaas Rockox (1560–1640), and in his possession circa 1613; depicted over the fireplace in the "great parlour" of his house in Antwerp in a painting by Frans Francken the Younger of circa 1630–35; listed in the inventory made after his death, and drawn up 19–20 December 1640, as in the "groote Saleth—Eene schilderye, olieverwe op panneel in syne lyste beteeckenende Samson ende Delilah, van dmaecxsel van den heer Rubens".

Perhaps in the possession of Jeremias Wildens, Antwerp, and listed in the inventory of 30 December 1653, drawn up after his death, as "Eenen Samson van Rubens".

Perhaps in the possession of Guill. Potteau, Antwerp, and listed in the inventory of 2 August 1692 drawn up after his death.

Acquired by Johann Adam Andreas, Prince of Liechtenstein (1662–1712) on 30 May 1700 from the Antwerp dealers Forchoudt. It had been the subject of correspondence between Marcus Forchoudt, in Vienna, acting on instructions of the Prince of Liechtenstein, and Guillaum Forchoudt in Antwerp between 1698–1699, and it is *likely to have been* the picture owned by Raetsheer Segers on the Mier. It was sent by Guillaum Forchoudt to Vienna by 17 June 1698, and after some doubts which were quickly dispelled, it was shown to the Prince by 5 September and negotiations for its purchase had begun. Listed in catalogues of the Liechtenstein Princely Collections of 1767, 1780 and 1873 (*but not attributed to Rubens*).

Sold by Johann II Prince of Liechtenstein in Paris, 1880.

Discovered in Paris, 1929.

Acquired from Van Diemen and Benedict by August Neuerburg, 22 Jan., 1930.[4]

As I turned the pages of the black-and-white catalogue, I came across an engraving (in mirror image) of the painting, by a seventeenth-century Dutch engraver named Jacob Matham. On the next page I noticed a second visual testimony of the original: *The Five Senses* by Frans Francken the Younger, now in the Alte Pinakothek in Munich. This painting was, in fact, a miniature representation of the interior of Rockox's great salon, with the original *Samson and Delilah* hanging over the fireplace. The quality of the photocopy made it hard to distinguish any of the details with clarity, but there was clearly a wealth of exciting material.

RESEARCH ON PROVENANCE

Eager to research the painting's provenance further, Siân, Steve, and I drew up a list of leads based on the Christie's catalogue. The catalogue listed the collection of the Prince of Liechtenstein, where the painting was reportedly included in 1767, 1780, and 1873. We had been told that the Liechtenstein catalogues were to be found in the National Art Library, housed in the Victoria and Albert Museum. We decided to send our most respectable operative, the prim and delicate-looking Siân.

Steve chose to visit the Art History Library of the City of Westminster, just behind Leicester Square. I went to the Warburg Library of the University of London, a place I had spent many happy hours doing research for my book *The Mysterious Fayum Portraits*. The Warburg had been the source of many wonderful revelations; I had often experienced delight in its day-lit basement as I stumbled across yet another secret of the Egyptian mummies.

I was fortunate to be allowed into this magical treasure-house, and once again it did not disappoint me.

Before long, I had found the carefully documented inventories of paintings from seventeenth-century Antwerp that had been compiled by the Belgian archivists J. Denucé and Dr Erik Duverger. Copies of these published inventories could only be found in extremely specialised art history libraries, but here they were, just a few bus stops away from home. I opened them with enormous excitement and leafed through the pages, scanning the unfamiliar Flemish words, hoping to find something I could understand.

Although I was totally unfamiliar with the language (despite being a quarter Flemish), I used numbers as my guide: dates that I could recognise. I found the year of Rockox's death, 1640 (it was easy to remember because it was the same year that his younger friend, Peter Paul Rubens, had also died). Were these the inventories of Jeremias Wildens, and of Guillaume Potteau? Did they contain mention of the original *Samson and Delilah*? I would need help with the translation, but I was proud of my Belgian ancestors for their meticulous record-keeping.

I was filled with excitement. A part of me wanted to rush outside into the sunlight and celebrate the find, dancing in Woburn Square—but I restrained myself and merely asked permission to photocopy the pages. Many books were too fragile to be put through the photocopiers, so I had to painstakingly copy the information I needed by hand—a task made even more laborious by the fact that I did not speak the language.

SIÂN'S DISCOVERY

The three of us re-convened for tea at Daquise, a Polish restaurant behind South Kensington station. I had used this charming haunt, filled with Poles and scruffy students, as a refuge since my days at the Slade. Siân grinned like a Cheshire cat as she dug through her bag for her notes. "We've got them!" She said triumphantly. "Why, what have you found?" I responded. She seemed even more excited than I was.

"All three of the Liechtenstein catalogues call it a Jan van den Hoecke. None of them says it's a Rubens". She handed me scraps of paper torn from her notebook and I scanned them excitedly, Steve craning over my shoulder.

"Why the hell do Christie's include it in the provenance then?" Demanded Steve. "Your guess is as good as mine!"

I interrogated Siân to ensure she had copied everything correctly. The three catalogues were respectively in German, Italian, and French, none of which she was fluent in. Even between us we couldn't make much of the texts, so we decided we would take the next few days to decipher them. In fact, the study of the Liechtenstein provenance was to take up many years of research, and I have come to the certain conclusion that Rubens's *Samson and Delilah* was never in the Liechtenstein Collection.

ANTWERP INVENTORIES

In the Christie's catalogue, we read about two seventeenth-century Antwerp Inventories. On translating and reading them, I could find no mention of a *Samson and Delilah* painting by Rubens, except in an inventory drawn up *after* the death of Rockox **[14]**.

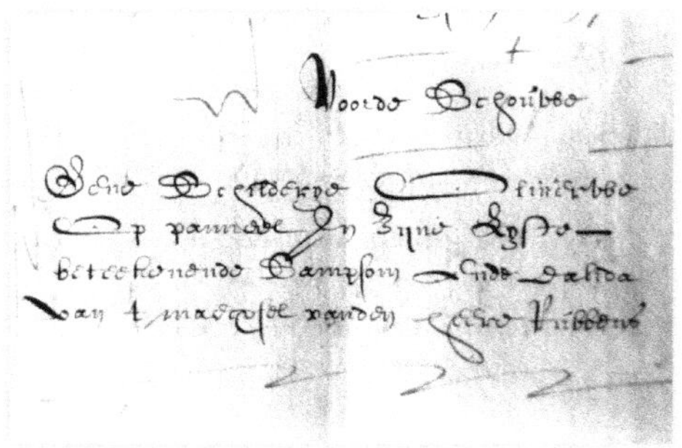

14. Inventory: Drawn after the death of Nicolaas Rockox and mentioning Rubens's *Samson and Delilah*.

THE TESTIMONY OF EYEWITNESSES

But we have something better: two eyewitnesses' visual record of the painting. First, Jacob Matham had in *c.*1613–5 produced two engravings of *Samson and Delilah*: in one, Delilah's hair cascades freely over her shoulders **[15]**, and in the other it is tied up, leaving the shoulders bare **[16]**. That both engravings were based on the original painting is confirmed by the presence of the same Latin inscription at the bottom right corner:

> To the most noble and serene Heer Nicolaas Rockox, Knight, at various times Burgomaster of Antwerp, lover of the fine arts, this image which has been engraved by myself in bronze, with care and attention, depicts the original work painted by the hand of the Master Peter Paul Rubens, which is on view in his house where it can be admired. Matha[m] L. M. D. D. [5]

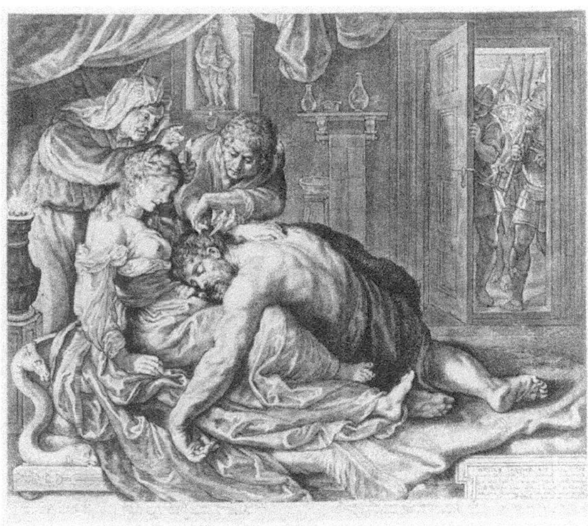

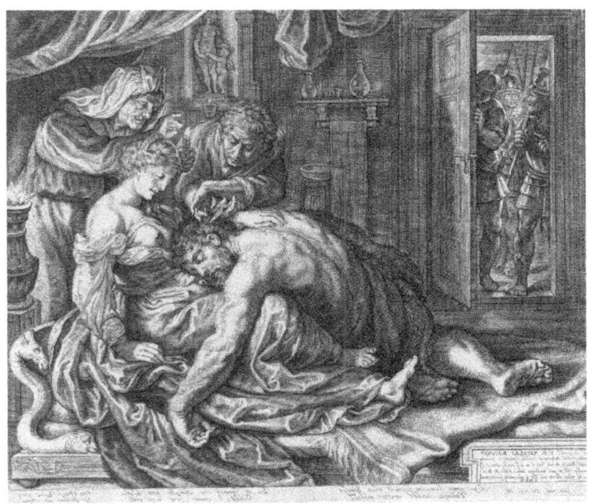

The Christie's catalogue had also led us to another historical record: twenty years later, Frans Francken II, a renowned artist who specialised in miniature renditions of paintings had included the lost *Samson and Delilah* in his oil painting *Banquet in the House of Nicolaas Rockox*. It was customary in the seventeenth century, long before the advent of photography, for collectors to have their art collection documented in paintings known as *Kunstkammeren* (literally translated as 'art rooms'). Since Rockox would have displayed the best works of his collection in his living room, a depiction of that room served as a kind of catalogue. Painted on panel, it survives to this day and hangs in the Alte Pinakothek in Munich. *Samson and Delilah* is seen right above the fireplace.

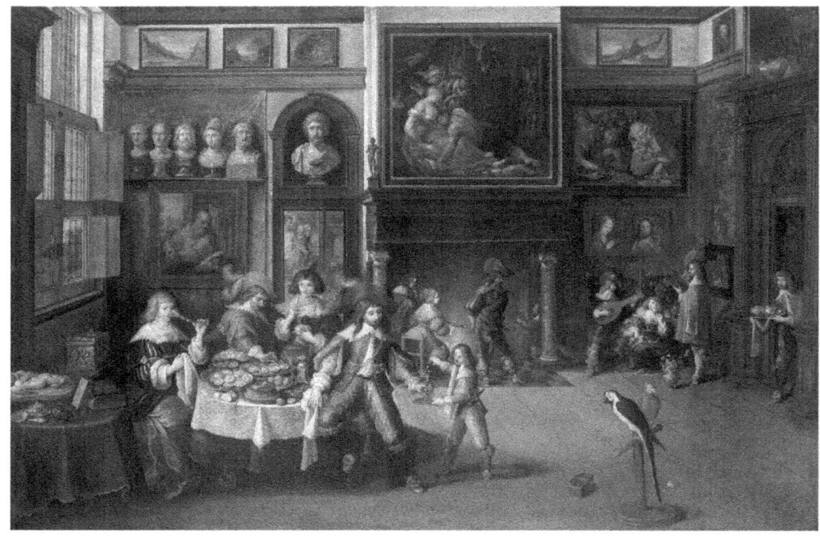

In Francken's rendering **[17]**, we have a record of the colours, the frame, and the architectural setting. Interestingly, we do not know the dimensions of Rockox's *Samson and Delilah*, and it is only from looking at Francken's depiction that we can quite reliably infer its size by comparing its proportions to the still existing fireplace. Rockox's house in the Keizerstraat, called The Golden Ring, has since 1977 been a museum open to the public, beautifully restored by the bank that owned it. The huge fireplace in the *groote saleth* is the only original feature that survives. In 1983, for the National Gallery's Acquisition in Focus exhibition, a replica of the setting in the Rockox House was created and the picture was reframed for the installation—even though Christie's had indicated that the frame the painting was sold with was the original.

ROCKOX INVENTORY

After the great mayor's death on 12 December 1640 at his home on the Keizerstraat, a full inventory of his art collection was drawn up. It was conducted in the presence of the town pastors (heirs to Rockox's furniture and wealth) and of his nephew, Adriaan van Heetvelde, who received this property among others. The inventory, drawn up on 19–20 December by the notary David van der Soppen, states:

> In the *groote Saleth* [great salon], an oil painting, on wood, framed, depicting *Samson and Delilah*, a work by Heer Rubens.

Balance of accounts of everything owned by the deceased, including furniture and all other belongings, as well as all outstanding debts owed to My Lord Nicolaas Rockox, knight and former burgomaster of this city, when he was living in this city of Antwerp.[6]

The itemised list that followed reads:

Settlement of Accounts
On 6 June 1641, and on the following days, all the furniture, fine art, paintings, and so on were sold by Peter van Fraeyenborch, acting for the official public auctioneer, Jan Lindemans.[7]

Six months later came another document that had curiously been omitted from all published provenance literature. We discovered it with the help of Jan Caluwaerts—a genealogist and expert in seventeenth-century Flemish inventories—in the former poorhouse known as 'Maagdenhuis', where I had earlier found Rockox's will and inventories. On one of them **[18, 19]** we find:

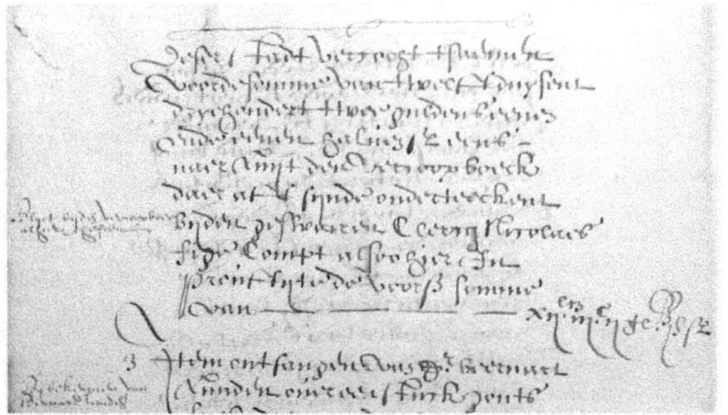
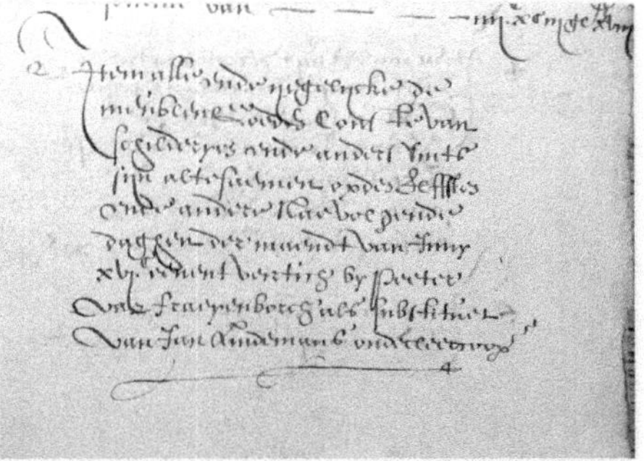

18, 19. Inventories: Two inventories drawn after Rockox's death, discovered through independent research.

The entire contents were sold for 12,302 guilders and 1/2 stuiver [a small coin], as attested by the bill of sale signed by the sworn clerk Nicolaes Fige. Thus the total profits of the sale are 12,302 guilders and 1/2 stuiver.[8]

This 1641 auction is the last verifiable written record of the original *Samson and Delilah* by Rubens, and we unfortunately have no information on the identity of its new owner (there exists no document that lists any of the buyers at that public auction). A note was scribbled in the margin:

This amount was cross-checked against and confirmed by the listing of the sale [9]

  OPENING PANDORA'S BOX

Jan exclaimed at the figure: it was extraordinarily high for the time, equivalent to the value of several palatial houses. Seventy-five years later, in 1714, at the death of Rockox's last heir, the house itself, The Golden Ring, fetched 10,200 guilders.

So Rubens's original *Samson and Delilah* was sold, along with the entire contents of Rockox's house, to the benefit of the poor, on, or just after, 6 June 1641. But who bought the painting? The original *Samson and Delilah* disappears in 1641, a fact that flatly discredits all speculations about other owners before 1929—such as the provenance claims made prior to the National Gallery's acquisition.

"WHEREABOUTS UNKNOWN"

Finally, I came across a text (dated 1904) by Max Rooses, conservator of the Museum Plantin-Moretus in Antwerp in the late nineteenth century. Rooses had spent years studying Rubens's life and work. There he notes:

> We know also that Rubens painted another picture for Rockox representing 'Samson betrayed by Delilah'. It was engraved by Jacob Matham, the only one of Rubens's creations which he reproduced. The picture's whereabouts are unknown, but in the engraving we find the same manner and even the same figures which we first became acquainted with in the 'Judith and Holofernes' engraved by Cornelis Galle: the male figure has the same colossal build and the same prominent muscles, the heroine has the same powerful shoulders, and finally the same old woman figures in both scenes. It is evidently, therefore, one of Rubens's earliest works.[10]

One phrase leapt off the page as I read this: "The picture's whereabouts are unknown"! Where, between its sale in 1641 and Rooses's claim, had it disappeared to? I also found another reference to the reproductions, this time by a German Rubens specialist, Rudolf Oldenbourg, in 1922:

> The original *Samson* [*and Delilah*] is unfortunately lost, but the small copy in Francken's painting at the Munich Pinakothek adds to what we know of it from the accurate engraving.[11]

Again, why didn't any serious scholar in the early part of the twentieth century know where such a significant painting was? I hurried back to the Christie's catalogue and its reported provenance: "Discovered in Paris in 1929". After the Rockox and before 1929, the only references to a namesake painting were in the Liechtenstein collection, which Siân had discovered concerned a Jan van den Hoeck. Where had the original Rubens that hung in Rockox's house gone after the 1641 public auction? Who purchased it, and what happened to it? Neither Christie's nor the National Gallery in their respective provenances, riddled with ambiguous repetitions of "perhaps" and "probably", nor for that matter the 1977 Antwerp Exhibition catalogue before them, have been helpful in answering those questions—on the contrary, they have served to obscure the painting's history even more.

NAER RUBENS (AFTER RUBENS)

Christie's had naturally researched the problem of gaps in provenance before offering the Neuerburg picture for sale in 1980. Their suggestion of what may have happened to Rockox's picture after 1640 begins:

> Perhaps in the possession of Jeremias Wildens, Antwerp, and listed in the inventory of 30 December 1653, drawn up after his death, as 'Eeren Sampson van Rubens' [a Samson by Rubens].[12]

The words "van Rubens" turned out to be deceptively straightforward. There are in fact two different mentions of "a Samson" in the long inventory drawn up at the death of the painter Wildens: one numbered 121 and the other 523. To complicate matters, two original versions of the inventory exist. And to complicate them further, two different authorities have quoted from the two different versions in their books. I spotted that the wording quoted by the eminent genealogist Erik Duverger in 1992 differed from that which had been given by J. Denucé, the Official Keeper of the Antwerp State Archives, in 1932. Later, Jan Caluwaerts, the genealogist whose help I had sought, tracked down the original documents, discovered the two different versions (something quite common for the period, it seems), and ordered photographs of the crucial details from both original copies [20, 21, 22].

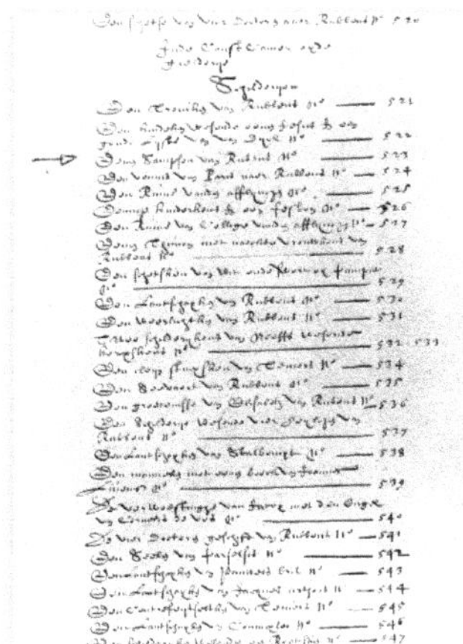

20, 21, 22. Inventories: The original documents (both versions).

In the first version, painting No. 121 is given as "naer Rubens" (*after* Rubens), and painting No. 523 as "van Rubens" (*by* Rubens). This is the version quoted by Denucé and relied on and selectively quoted by Christie's.

In the second version, on the other hand, No. 121 is a *Samson*, again "naer Rubens", only this time No. 523 is, *also* "naer Rubens" (*after* Rubens). This is the text that Duverger cites; he was writing more recently—after the compilation of the Christie's catalogue—therefore, one could reasonably assume that he chose the version of the two he believed to be the truer.

And, of course, even if all four mentions referred to <u>a</u> *Samson* by Rubens, that need not have been the one that concerns us: there are many paintings by Rubens of the biblical figure: Samson being captured by the Philistines, Samson being blinded, Samson and the lion, and drawings of Samson slaying a Philistine.

The Christie's catalogue's speculation continues, again preceded by "perhaps":

Perhaps in the possession of Guill. Potteau, Antwerp, and listed in the inventory of 2 August 1692 drawn up after his death.[13]

The Potteau inventory **[23]** is cited by Denucé. I didn't need to be fluent in Flemish to decipher the only reference to *Samson and Delilah.* "A copy after Rubens"—surely, one can only think that here the catalogue listing was misleadingly optimistic.

Inventory Guillaume POTTEAU (+1692)
City Archive of Antwerp ("Stadsarchief van Antwerpen": Venus-straat. 11, B-2000 Antwerp)
Notary E.H. Beres, register 2825 folio 237-verso

THE CHRISTIE'S PROVENANCE IN THE TWENTIETH CENTURY

From the Christie's catalogue we learn that NG6461 was "sold by Johann II Prince of Liechtenstein in Paris in 1880. [...] Discovered in Paris, in 1929"[14]. But I looked at the bibliography and concluded that it was impossible to substantiate either claim. Was it ever in the Liechtenstein Collection? I was not convinced. I was expecting some record to exist of this purported sale of 1880 in the Christie's catalogue bibliography, because the main auction house in Paris in the 1880s was the Hôtel Drouot, and documentation of these sales does exist—finding it should have just been a matter of scholarship. I decided to write to Reinhold Baumstark, Director (at that time) of the Liechtenstein Princely Collections, confident that all this uncertaintly would be cleared up when he replied. I didn't know that a reply would never come, at least not from the Director.

As for the painting's 'discovery' in 1929, there was no description of how, why, or by whom it was discovered. The Christie's catalogue continues: "acquired from Van Diemen and Benedict by August Neuerburg, 22 Jan., 1930"[15]. August Neuerburg, who bought the painting in 1930 from the German art dealers Van Diemen and Benedict, was a German tobacco industrialist and art collector. Again, no information on the circumstances of the Neuerburg purchase could be found in the bibliography. For such an important work by such a prominent artist, the available information was suspiciously sparse.

After its triumphant purchase by the National Gallery, NG6461 was put on display at the museum for a few days and then spent the next three years in their Conservation Department. Its re-emergence in 1983 was celebrated by a major exhibition, *Acquisition in Focus*, which was accompanied by booklet.

The information in the main body of the booklet was not terribly useful, but there was an interesting remark in the acknowledgements, made by the author Dr Christopher Brown, Curator of Dutch and Flemish Paintings at the National Gallery. After duly thanking the Rubenianum for their assistance, Brown wrote: "Under the terms of Ludwig Burchard's will, I had the privilege of consulting his manuscript notes on the *Samson and Delilah*"[16]. What were these manuscript notes? Might they be available to the public? The Rubenianum in Antwerp is the global centre of Rubens studies; it is heavily subsidised by the Belgian state and is home to the largest archive of material and research on Rubens, his life, and all works of his that are in existence. It also contains the personal library of Ludwig Burchard (1886–1960), the 'patron saint' of Rubens studies.

I was so excited to learn that Ludwig Burchard had initiated a monumental series, twenty-nine volumes strong, which is still being added to today. The work is called the *Corpus Rubenianum Ludwig Burchard*; it is an ambitious catalogue raisonné of the entire Rubens oeuvre, including copies from the school of Rubens, engravings, and so on. Volume *III / The Old Testament* was at that time in the process of being published (thankfully, the *Corpus* is published in English).

Siân, Steve, and I wrote a letter to the publishers requesting to see a preview of an entry in the forthcoming *III / The Old Testament* volume on the National Gallery's *Samson and Delilah* (NG6461). A few months later we received the typescript. Unfortunately, both the provenance and the literature were omitted. When the book came out a year later, in 1989, it did contain both the literature and the provenance, which concurred with the Christie's catalogue.

MAX ROOSES

One point in the *Corpus Rubenianum III / The Old Testament* provenance was particularly interesting. Most people would consider Max Rooses's claim of 1904 that the *Samson and Delilah* was a *tableau inconnu* (a painting with unknown whereabouts) to be rather significant. Not so the authors of this prestigious reference book. Not only do they list Rooses in their bibliography for NG6461—and not only do they ignore his mention of the *tableau inconnu*—they even record him as attributing the painting that now hangs in the Gallery to Rubens. But Rooses had clearly written that the painting was lost! What sort of woolly scholarship was this? The more I found out, the more questions I had. I continued my research by delving into the information provided by Hans Gerhard Evers in his 1943 monograph *Rubens und sein Werk: neue Forschungen*[17], which provided a full analysis of NG6461 while it was in Neuerburg's collection.

1977 ANTWERP RUBENS EXHIBITION

Ludwig Burchard's opinion carried—and continues to carry—enormous weight in academic circles. When, in 1977, the city of Antwerp celebrated the four-hundredth anniversary of Rubens's birth, the Royal Museum of Fine Arts staged an enormous exhibition of Rubens's paintings, oil sketches, and drawings. Among these they included NG6461 (which had, in the meantime, been inherited by the art dealer August Neuerburg's daughter, Mrs Margaret Köser), thereby tacitly accepting it as genuine. In the catalogue, jointly written by a team of experts from the Rubenianum—including Frans Baudouin—and the Royal Museum of Fine Arts, the picture is confidently ascribed to Rubens and given a Liechtenstein provenance, apparently merely on the word of Burchard and R. A. d'Hulst, of the Rubenianum in Antwerp, author of the *Old Testament* volume (1989).

We read there: "Nicolaas Rockox, bourgmestre d'Anvers, décédé en 1640; prince de Liechtenstein, Vienne; A. Neuerburg, Hambourg",[18] as though the painting had casually passed directly from one owner to another, leaving no room for doubt about the matter. Yet, in his catalogue for the newly opened Rockox House museum, written in the same year, Baudouin makes no mention of a Liechtenstein provenance:

> For a long time the composition of this work was merely known through the print by Matham. The painting itself reappeared for the first time in 1929 and was recognised by Ludwig Burchard as being the chimneypiece painting of Rockox's house.[19]

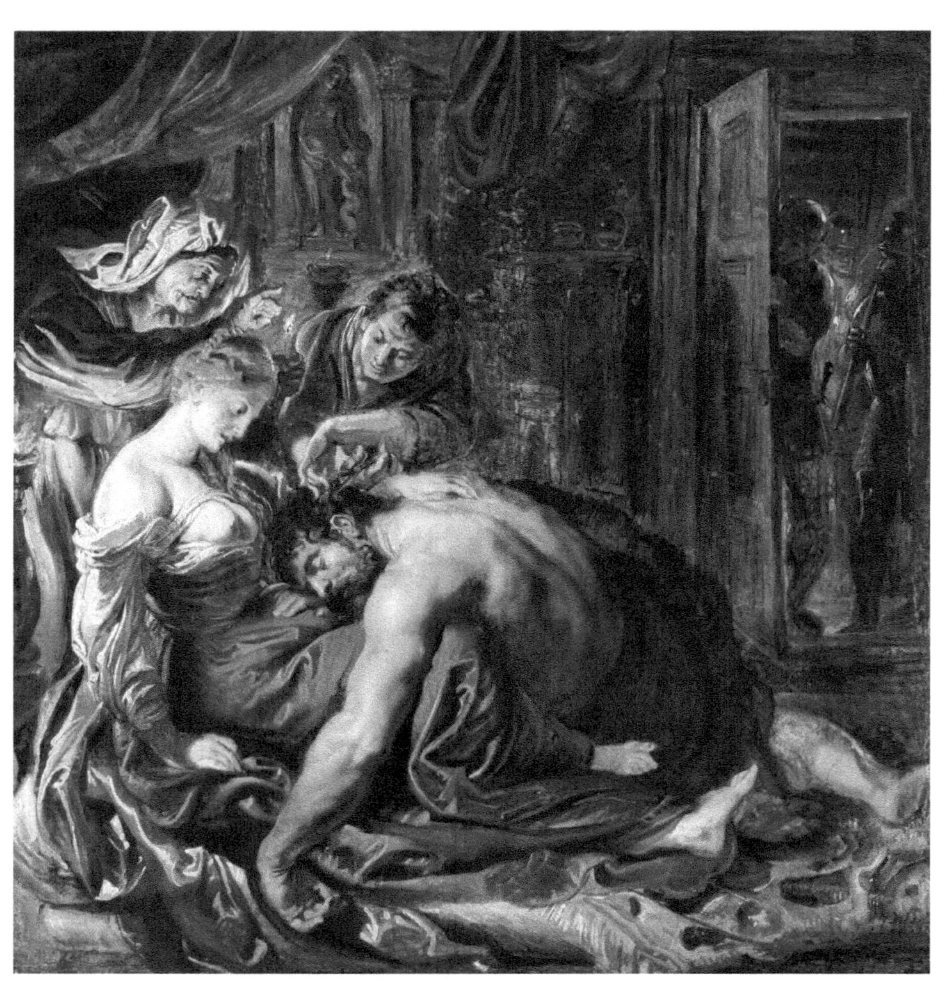

Samson's Missing Toes

Perhaps the most extraordinary feature of the painting is the omission of Samson's toes. It is not that the panel has been cut down (width-wise), as one would think at first. Behind the frame, the foot simply stops at the edge of the paint.

THE SPURIOUS *MODELLO*

The Christie's auction catalogue states that there is an oil sketch (*modello*) by Rubens for *Samson and Delilah*, as well as a "preparatory drawing [...] in the collection of Professor J. Q. van Regteren Altena"[1]. They are both mentioned in support of the painting's authenticity. However, there is no known provenance for either of these works prior to the twentieth century. What is the history of these two objects, and how can we know that they are authentic?

Let us first look at the oil sketch **[24]**. Rubens would prepare rough versions of a final piece on hardwood panels (which would oftentimes end up differing significantly from the finished work) to give his prospective client an idea of the composition and the proposed colour scheme. Such a small-scale painting—a work of art in its own right—is called a *modello*, from the Italian for 'model'. In English it is termed an 'oil sketch', but there need be nothing sketchy about it. Particularly in the case of Rubens, such works are in a sort of calligraphic shorthand that is highly developed and articulate: certain vital details appear as vividly in the *modello* as in the finished work. Today, the original *modelli* are among the works indisputably by Rubens's own hand.

The *Samson and Delilah modello*, however, comes shrouded in a mystery at least as opaque as that which envelops the finished painting. It was also sold by Christie's and is presently in

24. Peter Paul Rubens
Samson and Delilah
(the 'spurious' *modello*).

the Cincinnati Art Museum. John Herbert, a former employee of the firm, later wrote in his sizzling kiss-and-tell account *Inside Christie's*:

> The circuitous way by which the modello came for sale is an object lesson for both auctioneers and museums. The modello had been bought sixty years earlier by a lady in a Yorkshire antique shop for a few shillings. Her step-granddaughter, who still wishes to remain anonymous, told me that it had been bought mainly for its gilt frame, the panel being badly cracked.[2]

After an unsuccessful attempt to extract a written attribution and evaluation from Sotheby's and Christie's, the dejected owner decided to take it to the National Gallery, where she was advised by an employee, who also mysteriously reassured her that Rubens had never painted a large picture of the same subject, to take it back to Christie's. If this anecdote is true, the National Gallery employee evidently trusted the expertise of Christie's more than his own. Back at Christie's, the owner of the *modello* finally struck it lucky. In the entrance hall, she bumped into David Carritt, an employee at Christie's at the time, who enthusiastically "recognised it for what it was" (whatever that may have been) and "the delighted vendor left it for sale"[3]. The sale took place on 25 November 1966.

CARRITT VS SEWELL

David Carritt, was rumoured to have "the best eye in England". However, another Christie's employee, Brian Sewell, later art critic for the *Evening Standard*, claimed that it was he, and not Carritt, who made this great discovery. Sewell made the following statement: "Then suddenly a boy from the Front Counter arrived with a panel picture, virtually 'two pieces of timber'. [...] I took one look at it and knew in my bones it was by Rubens"[4].

A host of influential curators and collectors passed through the viewing rooms of Christie's in advance of the November sale, including Sir Oliver Millar (Keeper of the Queen's Pictures), Michael Jaffé (the great Rubens expert), and Gregory Martin (Assistant Keeper at the National Gallery at the time), together with the-then Director of the Gallery, Sir Philip Hendy. Fourteen years later, Martin (by then working for Christie's) would sell the 'original' painting purportedly 'based' on this *modello* to the

National Gallery at the 1981 Christie's auction. All the experts were thoroughly impressed. Sir Oliver said of another *modello* attributed to Rubens in the same sale—a *modello* of the *The Judgement of Paris*—that "it smelt of Rubens"[5].

One might think, given that the sketch bore the initials "P P R", that it perhaps shouldn't take a genius to make the attribution. But the step from recognition to authentication is not a small one: according to the eminent Rubens scholar Arnout Balis,

> [s]ignatures are only of limited value here, since Rubens seldom signed his works (and may—theoretically—have included studio works in that selection), and requirements put down in contracts or claims made by the artist are open to interpretation, since 'authorship' apparently was not a rigorously circumscribed category.[6]

JULIUS HELD

In 1980, another great authority on Rubens, Julius Held, published *The Oil Sketches of Peter Paul Rubens*[7], a definitive work on Rubens's *modelli*. This exhaustive two-volume catalogue included both a colour and a black-and-white photograph of the *modello* of *Samson and Delilah* that had appeared at Christie's in 1966. Held cites a reference in an inventory drawn up after the death of Joannes Philippus Happart of Antwerp in 1686: "Item, a sketch by Mr Rubens of *Samson and Delilah*". In the *Corpus Rubenianum III / The Old Testament*, the authors recycle this reference three times in order to supply three different *modelli* with provenance: No. 31b, *Samson Asleep in Delilah's Lap*; No. 32, *Samson Taken by the Philistines*; and No. 33, *The Blinding of Samson*.[8]

MISSING SIDES?

The problems with the *modello* do not end with its invented provenance. First, it is the only known sketch attributed to Rubens that is on a soft wood (conifer) rather than hardwood (like oak) which he used for all others.[9] Secondly, the figure of Samson is abruptly cut off at the toes, which, while it retrospectively serves to corroborate the National Gallery's authenticity claim, becomes further complicated by the fact that the *modello* may have had further pieces of wood attached at either side. The photograph in the Christie's catalogue for the *modello* sale (25 November 1966, Lot 66), indeed, shows additional painted strips on either side;

the dimensions given are 21 × 23¼ in. (53 × 59 cm)—much wider than the 51.8 × 50.6 cm provided in Held's 1980 catalogue (Held omitted the two side strips which, by that point, had disappeared). With these strips in place—judging from the blurry illustration—there was room for Samson's toes, though they appear to have been outlined rather than painted. Comparing the sketch with the National Gallery painting, Held observes that, "whereas the sketch is almost square, the finished painting is distinctly wider than high".[10] The proportions of the right-hand side of the full-scale picture are curious; it is almost as if the toe-clipped version of the square modello was stretched out at the right to fit a more 'correct' format.

The various reproductions of the *modello* are puzzling. The photographs in the Christie's catalogues of 1966 (sale of the *modello*) and 1980 (sale of the full-scale painting) show the complete *modello* with strips on either side, and all of Samson's toes. In Held's book, however, the strips (and toes) are missing, and the *modello* is almost a perfect square. The colour illustration shows deep cracks running vertically down the surface, seemingly separating the work into three planks (corresponding to Held's description in his catalogue), whereas the black-and-white photo has no cracks at all. And the illustrations in both Christie's catalogues show the *modello* cracked in completely different places from those in the Held colour plate.

HELD CHANGES HIS MIND

While it is admirable for scholars to revise their opinions, one cannot help being puzzled by Held's radical change of position regarding the question of the missing toes. In his *Oil Sketches*, he writes of the *modello*: "the toes of Samson are missing, which is an unlikely manner for Rubens to handle such a detail"[11]—a clear statement from a great Rubens expert. This led him to "consider it likely that the sketch has lost small sections on either side"[12]. By 1989, however, he arrived to the opposite view: that the strip at the right of the *modello* had been added later (with a strip to the left for visual balance) by someone who had 'missed' the toes. At the time of writing his catalogue, Held explains, he thought half a foot looked a bit awkward; but he didn't miss the toes in the London painting, where almost the entire sole of the foot is visible. Yet he also says he had seen NG6461 at the Rubens exhibition in Antwerp in 1977—before completing his *Oil Sketches*—and been "bowled over"[13]. Might the fact that the painting was "the sensation of the exhibition" have affected his awareness of the 'unlikely' handling?

ANOTHER RED HERRING

The other twentieth-century discovery (the third, if you count the full painting itself) is a pen-and-brush and brown ink drawing which was discovered and exhibited in 1933 **[25]**. The *Corpus Rubenianum* authors give its provenance, frankly, as "Unknown".[14]

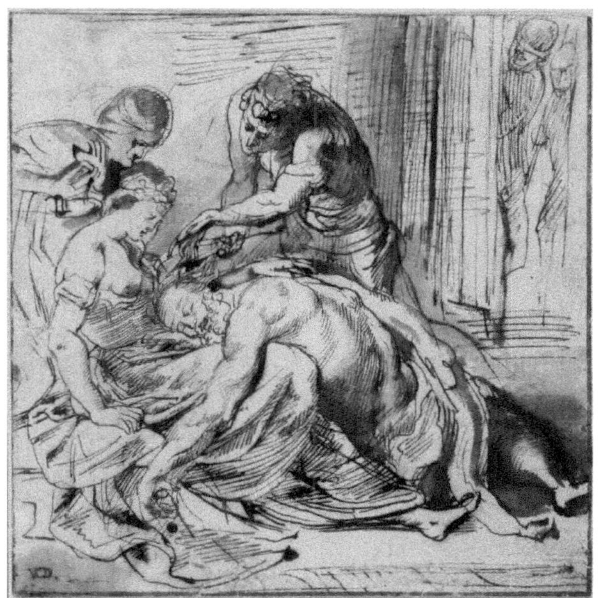

25. Peter Paul Rubens
Samson and Delilah (possibly another misattribution).

It is now, as we learnt from the *Samson and Delilah* Christie's sale catalogue, in the collection of Prof J. Q. van Regteren Altena in Amsterdam.[15] This reference of a related drawing has been used to buttress the authenticity of the National Gallery picture: in it, too—as has already been noted—Samson is toeless. Unusually, it is varnished, something that prevents ink analysis; the quality of the drawing is very poor; and its lack of provenance is not reassuring—altogether, perhaps, not a very substantial peg on which to hang any authentication. Overall, this is an unconvincing piece of evidence for the authenticity of the National Gallery painting, as its provenance, like the *modello*'s, is totally unsubstantiated. Both objects only muddy the waters of serious research. Personally, after many years of study, I believe they were both fabricated in the twentieth century.

Fortunately, we do not have to rely on the dubious evidence of the *modello* or the drawing for a description of the original *Samson and Delilah* that Rubens painted for Rockox for his great parlour. We have something much better: a visual record made by two reliable contemporary eyewitnesses: the Dutch engraver Jacob Matham and Frans Francken II.

Both renderings of the real *Samson and Delilah* were unquestionably made during Rockox's and Rubens's lifetime, and Matham's engraving shows (i) Samson's foot complete; (ii) his extended toes aligning with the right edge of the door in the background; and (iii) a comfortable space between that alignment and the right-hand side of the picture, balancing the space between Delilah's arm and the left side of the picture. In the National Gallery version, the whole figure of Samson is shifted to the right in relation to the background, and his foot hits the edge as if slipping out of a preordained frame. This alone, without further evidence, would seem to me conclusive proof that the painting that is hanging in Room 18 of the National Gallery is not the same that hung over Rockox's fireplace.

Matham's engraving bears an inscription where he dedicates his print to Nicolaas Rockox, and states that the Rubens painting of which his print is a copy could be admired in Rockox's home. Rubens himself would inevitably have seen the print as well; and he is known to have been extremely fastidious when he vetted engravings of his paintings.

It is also known that Francken was working on Rockox's commission. There are, indeed, minor differences between the engravings and Francken's painting. The proportions of the image are wider; the top of the niche on the back wall behind the statue of Venus and Cupid is incomplete; the shapes of the brazier behind Samson's back are different (they are braziers, emitting light, not a bowl and ewer); and Matham shows a carved lioness's head at the bottom of Delilah's bedhead. But all agree on the completeness and relative position of Samson's foot. Francken might conceivably have taken a liberty, but Matham's engraving is actually dedicated to Rockox: why would he make his composition so different from the one Rockox saw every day? And how could his 'revision' (and that of Francken) not look like criticisms of Rubens, if the master had decided to extend the foot and cut off the toes? Why should Rubens have accepted Matham's engraving?

To cut off part of a protagonist's body in the way we see in the London painting, especially when on all other sides the triangular figure group has ample space around it, would be absolutely uncharacteristic of Rubens's work. If in the original painting the toes actually *were* cut off, we would have to consider this a brilliantly iconoclastic compositional decision by Rubens. Why would both Matham and Francken subvert it in such an obvious way?

But Rubens doesn't chop bits off. Even if the Matham and Francken copies did not exist, I think there would be grave reasons for being unhappy with this cutting off of the foot. The idea of presenting a fragment of a body or of some other important form in a picture, is totally foreign to the classical tradition in which Rubens worked. Not until the mid-nineteenth century, with the advent first of Japanese prints and then of photography, did painters make a point of showing bodies arbitrarily incomplete. It became a favourite device of the Impressionists, contributing to a feeling of spontaneity, of fortuitous accident, and therefore of *real* life—though one might think that such a suggestion of movement would hardly be appropriate for a sleeping figure whatever the conventions of the period (some art historians have seen it as one of the defining characteristics of Modernism). Is it not surprising that none of the experts who have views on NG6461 seems to have considered—if only to reject it—this elementary point? Even though in many respects Rubens's technique was revolutionary—and in some ways he was a Modernist *avant la lettre*—it stretches the limits of art historical credulity that Rubens would undercut the impact to Samson's fate by cutting off his toes as well as his hair. Rubens had a very strong sense of drama, and would surely not distract the viewer's attention from the crucial haircutting by raising questions about toe-cutting.

TRIP TO MUNICH TO SEE THE FRANCKEN PAINTING

On 6 May 1987, I woke up with a sense of renewed conviction. I went to our studio and announced to Siân and Steve: "We're going to Munich this weekend to see the Francken painting".

The expedition was reminiscent of Antonioni's *Blow-Up,* where the protagonist enlarges part of a photograph he has taken in order to reveal a murderer. I realised that, if we were to find any real clues to the identity of the painter, we would have to go back to the visual testimony of the eyewitnesses who had visited 'the scene of the crime', as it were. Luckily, unlike in the National

Gallery, photography was at the time permitted at the Munich Alte Pinakothek, so I packed my cameras, bought three plane tickets to Frankfurt, and off we went.

From Frankfurt we took the train to Munich. Fortunately, the Francken painting was on display. The actual size of the *Samson and Delilah* painting-within-a-painting is no bigger than an A5 sheet of paper. That is, admittedly, tiny—but Francken was a meticulous painter copyist. His depictions are so accurate that they were frequently used for documentation.[16] We took a great many photos of his painting of Rockox's parlour, so that we could blow them up and better examine all the details. In Francken's painting, Samson's foot was there in its entirety. And Francken's work tallied completely with the Matham engraving in its composition; it was just subtler and more 'Rubenesque' in its colour scheme.

DETAILED COMPARISON WITH FRANCKEN MINIATURE

It was essential to make detailed comparisons between the Rockox *Samson and Delilah* as depicted by Francken **[26]**, and the version hanging in the National Gallery **[27]**. There are differences between the two: differences in composition, colour, and tonal values.

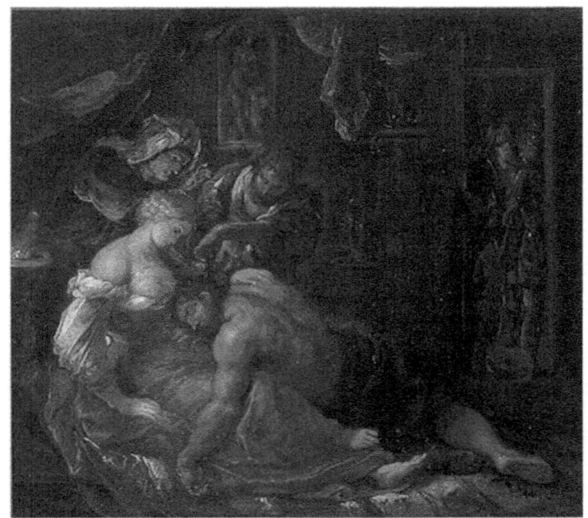
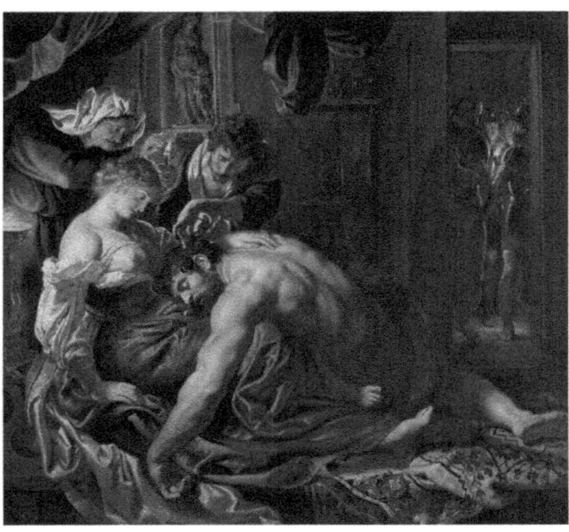

26, 27. Comparison: *Samson and Delilah* as depicted in Francken's *Supper at the House of the Burgomaster Rockox* (left); and NG6461 (right).

Beginning with the Francken, the overall effect is noticeably different to that of NG6461. The Francken picture-within-a-picture features warmer colours, where light sources are directional. The torch on its stand, the candle flame, the little flame in the niche illuminating the statuette of Venus and Cupid, and the torch of the Philistines at the door all cast the sort of soft illumination typical of a flame. In the National Gallery version, on the other hand, the scene is stage-lit from the front with a cold, harsh light that overpowers all the depicted light sources and flattens the scene.

The colour palette is, also, very different. Where the colour harmony in the Francken rendering produces an integrated whole, the more jarring colours in the National Gallery version strike a discordant note. In the Francken, Delilah's dress is a warm red ochre with vermilion highlights (Rubens's trademark red), whereas, in the other, it is replaced by a harsh alizarin crimson that competes for the viewer's attention with the equally harsh whites and yellows of the garments, the garish purple, and the glaring browns and pinks of the male and female skins. This optical struggle distracts the viewer and draws attention away from the important event that is taking place, especially since the dull brown of the background is also lit up because the pale underpainting (*imprimatura*) is showing through the entire surface.

In the Francken copy, the background is subdued, focussing attention on the central figures, and allowing the protagonists to stand out like a sculpted group. Rudolf Oldenbourg in 1922 believed that the original was lost, but of the Francken he observed: "the effect of the contrast of light and dark (still in the manner of Caravaggio) was very strong"[17]. That is to say, the scene took place in the dark and the directional light played only on the figures in the foreground, which accentuated their three-dimensionality. As we see in Francken's depiction, the group of figures seems lit by the windows to the left in such a way that a viewer standing in the room would have had the impression that the painted figures were three-dimensional. Oldenbourg's observation could not have been made about NG6461, with its over-illuminated background and resultant lack of depth.

Samson's back, which is a warm red colour in Francken's painting, is in the National Gallery version a green closer to *terre verte*, and heavy dark shadows appear on Delilah's elaborate clothing where none exist in the Francken version. Francken might conceivably have subordinated the colours of the paintings he was copying to his own overall colour scheme, yet the little replica has a recognisably Rubensian colour harmony. It is this typical colour scheme that makes it stand out as a Rubens among the other paintings in Francken's 'gallery'.

There are also major compositional differences between the two paintings. First, let us look at the position of the old woman holding the candle. In both the Francken painting and the

Matham engraving, her head is almost directly above Delilah's, so that the flame of her candle stands out brilliantly against the dark of the barber's shoulder. In the National Gallery version, her head is set further back, so that the candle is lost against the overexposed brown background. Her altered position also disturbs the relationship between the four heads. In Francken's version they are closely grouped, once again concentrating attention on the figures as a whole, an effect helped by the subtle lighting. The National Gallery picture loses this quality, appearing disjointed by comparison. Other points of departure include the perspective of the doorway being completely different; the area that the carpet takes up being much larger; and the hanging drapery above the old woman's head being almost unrecognisable between the two versions.

These differences, however, are relatively insignificant compared to the most startling discrepancy: Samson's missing toes. NG6461 shows Samson's outstretched foot positioned well to the right of the imaginary line of the door if we extended it downwards, with the toes missing, severed by the edge of the panel. Francken's copy clearly depicts the foot within this imaginary line and in its entirety, with the addition of a considerable gap between it and the panel's edge. This completes the powerful pyramidal composition of the figure group, which is crowned by the arch of the alcove in the background; the top of this arch is also severed in the National Gallery painting.

We bought lots of literature from the Alte Pinakotek, including a little biography of Francken. On the train back to Frankfurt, we were laughing, relaxing, and inventing limericks mocking the fake painting. I started reading Francken's biography. I already knew that he was a friend and contemporary of Rubens, a famous *Kunstkammer* painter renowned for his absolute precision and attention to detail. What I did not know until that moment was that Francken was baptised on 6 May 1581 and died on 6 May 1642: the exact same date I had decided that we should embark on this mission to Munich. I was astounded by this coincidence. As with many other events that took place during the course of my research, I wondered if any of it was just serendipity. It was almost as though Frans Francken was trying to tell me: "I painted the original. Come and see for yourself!"

5

David and Goliath

THE WIMBLEDON LECTURE

Our meeting with Francken in Munich was decisive. Back at Wimbledon School of Art, the end of the academic year was approaching. We felt a great excitement and a wish to share our finds with our fellow students. Our request to give a lecture on the subject was granted cordially. The Art History Department at Wimbledon was outstanding. Many of our teachers were Courtauld Institute-trained and published authors.

We were given the amphitheatre for two hours. We had succeeded in advertising the lecture around the School, and the room was packed. Everyone was there, teaching staff and students alike. We made a video of our presentation that lasted about an hour and a half, showing slides that compared the National Gallery picture and its details with Rubens originals. The room was electrified.

After we had presented our case, several art historians, painters, and tutors came up to talk with us. They all gave suggestions as to what else we could do to definitively prove our case. Some said they would be going to see the picture again soon after, while others suggested that we start a petition. We thought it was a good idea, but ultimately decided against it. In retrospect, it would have been great to have buttressed our case with the consensus of over 150 people from the visual arts, including some art historians, all in agreement over the evident flaws in the National Gallery painting. We couldn't have had a more sympathetic audience.

REACTIONS AND RETALIATIONS

The first indication of what was in store for us came three days later. I was going back to my studio from the cafeteria when I bumped into an art professor. She was a slim woman with waist-long blonde hair and wearing high-heeled boots, much younger than me—probably in her early thirties. As our paths crossed, without even turning to look at me, she said: "I would put that Rubens thing away, if I were you, because you might end up in court". She strode off without stopping. I knew that she was friendly with some prominent art restorers—she had hinted as much to one of the other students. Her objection came as no surprise. That was the first taste of menace. Much worse intimidation was to come later. I thought to myself: "To hell with you! I refuse to be intimidated". But somewhere in the back of my mind the thought had been planted that perhaps I didn't have the right to question great institutions like the National Gallery.

JOANNA WOODALL AND JULIUS HELD

One of the people that came to find us after our lecture, Valerie Holman, an art history lecturer, recommended that we contact a Rubens expert and friend of hers, Joanna Woodall. She taught seventeenth-century Dutch art at the Courtauld Institute. A few days later, we agreed to meet Joanna at the National Gallery. After we pointed out all the flaws that we had found in the *Samson and Delilah*, she was convinced on a visual level that the painting was indeed quite problematic. We sat at the National Gallery cafeteria and discussed our plan of action.

Joanna proposed that she should write to Julius Held, then Art History Professor Emeritus at Columbia University. Held was already very old and one of the three most prominent Rubens experts at the time—the other two being Michael Jaffé (Director of the Fitzwilliam Museum in Cambridge), and R. A. d'Hulst (of the Rubenianum). As promised, Joanna wrote to Professor Held on our behalf:

> While these students fully accept the attribution of the design of this picture to Rubens, they question whether it was actually executed by him. As you may imagine, I was initially sceptical about this heretical suggestion. However, having listened to the students' arguments and discussed the execution at length with them in front of the picture, I have gradually come to the conclusion that their case deserves consideration. They are visually sensitive and highly trained and, unlike me, not inhibited by the weight of established art historical opinion.[1]

She told him about our research and enclosed some black-and-white detail photos of the painting, which we had purchased from the National Gallery shop. These pictures were very precious to us, as they had to be specially ordered. Joanna's letter went on:

> The second point primarily concerns the omission of Samson's toes from the National Gallery painting. The students recognise the similarity of the National Gallery picture to the oil sketch in Cincinnati, where the toes are also missing, but they also note your comment on this sketch that since the omission is not characteristic of Rubens, the panel may have lost small sections on either side.
>
> As the National Gallery painting does not appear to have been cut, it seems surprising that in both Jacob Matham's print and Frans Franken II's painting after Rockox's picture in his Picture Gallery of Nicolas Rockox (Munich), the whole of Samson's foot is included and in a quite different relationship to the door.[2]

Professor Held's reply to Woodall was quite extraordinary and in equal measure unexpected. Apart from the fact that he doubled down on his conviction of Rubens's authorship and the sheer brilliance of the painter's artistic accomplishment, he chose not to engage with, let alone convincingly answer, any of our criticisms regarding the lack of provenance, the missing foot, or any other objection. Joanna Woodall gave us his letter and, quoting her unequivocal trust in Held's authority, politely bowed out of the whole affair.

6

Blood Is Thicker Than Water

FIRST VISIT TO ANTWERP

I decided it was time to visit Antwerp. I intended to pay tribute to the artist whom I adored and felt such solidarity for. The fervour with which I had thrown myself into the 'fake' Rubens affair was inexplicable to myself and puzzling to those around me.

I also wanted to visit the home of Nicolaas Rockox. Maybe the fireplace in his great parlour, over which the original painting hung, would provide a critical piece of the puzzle. I was also eager to see in real life the famous altarpieces in Antwerp's Cathedral of Our Lady, *The Elevation of the Cross* and *The Descent from the Cross*, which Rubens painted just after his *Samson and Delilah*.

BRUSSELS—THE SCHEEPERS FAMILY

In June 1989, I set off by car for Antwerp via Brussels. I had another reason for wanting to visit Belgium: my mother was half Belgian. Her father, Émile Scheepers, had come to Athens in 1898 at the age of nineteen with his father, Zacharias Maria Arthur Scheepers, one of three engineers representing a company from Brussels that built bridges and railways, Ponts et Chaussées. The Greek Prime Minister, Charilaos Trikoupis, had commissioned my great-grandfather and his colleagues to build the first railroads in Greece. Zacharias's wife, Catherine Maas, was from Luxembourg: she spoke German with her children and grandchildren and French with her husband. This led the grandchildren, my mother's generation, to believe that they were Walloons, French-speaking Belgians.

The Scheepers never left Greece, and gradually my family lost touch with its Belgian roots. My uncle Arthur, my mother's youngest brother, had at some point burned the Scheepers family tree, proclaiming that he felt Greek and didn't want to know about the Belgians. As far as we knew, our Belgian ancestors came from Brussels, and I wanted to see whether I could track down any of my distant relatives.

JAN CALUWAERTS

When I arrived in Brussels, I headed for the National Archives. I explained to the archivist that I was looking for a genealogist to trace my family history. "If you're lucky, Mr Caluwaerts will be in today", she replied.

And lucky I was. Jan Caluwaerts, a tall, soft-spoken man in his early thirties, appeared from the back room. His scholarly air belied a martini-dry wit. Jan was happy to accept my commission and agreed to trace my family as far back as he could. He promised to send me the results of his research in August that year.

BEAUTIFUL ANTWERP

As I left Brussels behind, I coasted through Antwerp Berchem, a film-set façade of buildings whose layered roofs rose like a row of wedding cakes dusted with chocolate. Shop windows sparkled with diamonds. Antwerp has dominated the diamond trade since the sixteenth century; moreover, it has always done a roaring trade in textiles, copper, and silver, and it boasted the first international commodity exchange in Europe. During the sixteenth and seventeenth centuries, the city also evolved into one of the greatest cultural centres of Western Europe. In 1566, Guicciardini counted some 300 artists in Antwerp, almost twice the number of bakers the city had.[1] By the early seventeenth century, Antwerp had become renowned worldwide for painting, and no painter had a more glorious reputation than Peter Paul Rubens. Antwerp has been known as 'Rubens's city' ever since.

"For me, Rubens is the perfect Belgian"[2], wrote Conrad Busken Huet in 1879. The veneration of Rubens as a symbol of Flemish cultural heritage goes back to the late eighteenth century. Since Belgium did not achieve independence until 1830, the need to establish a strong national identity, politically and culturally, was acute. Thus, "Rubens and Antwerp became intertwined, so that Rubens's fame was also reflected upon Antwerp and on the United Kingdom of the Netherlands. In Rubens's international reputation people saw a useful instrument to boost national self-esteem"[3].

I paused to admire the Antwerpen-Centraal station, a fabulous vault of steel and glass created at the turn of the twentieth century. Its entrance hall looked more like a ballroom than a waiting room. Orthodox Jews in baggy black coats climbed aboard a tram that rattled off down the street. The boulevards narrowed into a labyrinth of cobbled lanes as I neared the old city centre. Steeples and spires stood watch above the rooftops like pious sentinels. My hotel overlooked the Groenplaats, or 'Green Square', once the town cemetery. Antwerp's forefathers had been dug up to make way for an underground car park, and the square was lined with cafés, lace shops, and tram-tracks, all overshadowed by the tallest spire of all—the Cathedral of Our Lady. The great master's presence was immediately obvious: a statue of Rubens has stood in the Groenplaats since 1840. Until then, a giant crucifix stood on its site—proof that Rubens had achieved the status of a god in Antwerp.

I went for a walk around town. I gravitated towards the cathedral—so majestic that it seemed to exert a magnetic force. Its Gothic turrets and spires reminded me of those miniature Giacometti sandcastles we spent whole afternoons constructing as children, dribbling the sand through our fingers, only to watch with a mixture of disappointment and delight as waves washed them away. But this structure was built to last—successive buildings and extensions seamlessly joined together, turret heaped upon turret, dome upon dome, growing grander and taller with each additional architectural flourish. Biblical scenes of stained glass glinted in the gloaming.

A handsome nude stood in the middle of Grote Markt, his bronze contours weathered green. He appeared to be hurling a severed hand at some unsuspecting passer-by. This is Silvius Brabo, the Roman hero who freed Antwerp from the clutches of Druon Antigoon, a giant who lived in the Het Steen, a fairy-tale castle on the banks of the River Scheldt. Antigoon terrorised ships entering the city by demanding extortionate tolls. If the crew refused to pay him, he would cut off their hands. Brabo challenged Antigoon, cut off his right hand, and flung it into the Scheldt. This is allegedly how the city got its name: Antwerpen is short for 'Hantwerpen' (to throw a hand), and the symbol of the city is still a little hand.

I strolled down to the Scheldt, along whose shores those intrepid sea dogs had sailed into the harbour of Antwerp, the third largest port in the world. I climbed up onto the broad waterfront promenade, and looked back over the city's rooftops. Following the border of blue mooring stones, I marvelled at the harbour, a seamless blend of old-fashioned charm and contemporary design so typical of this city, until the chimes of the cathedral beckoned me back into the maze of alleyways.

I half-expected gentlemen in stockings and plumed hats to leap out at me, but was greeted instead by stylish locals gliding about on bicycles, and endless boutiques flashing all manner of desirables: chocolates, rare books, clothes, and antiques. Seductive little beer gardens and restaurants decked with flowers nestled between them. I succumbed to the temptation to stop and simply stare at the Hendrik Conscienceplein, an Italianate square walled on one side by the seventeenth-century Jesuit monastery (now the Municipal Library) and on the other by the church of St Carolus Borromeo, the first Jesuit Church in Antwerp, whose baroque façade was largely designed by Rubens.

After his return from Italy in 1608, Rubens was invited to decorate both the interior and exterior of many of the city's churches that had been laid bare by the religious clashes of the previous century. In the throes of the Counter-Reformation, ecclesiastical architecture became critically important for Antwerp, the last bulwark of Catholicism poised precariously on the borders of the Protestant north. Locals hailed the Jesuit church as the eighth wonder of the world. As well as the altarpiece, Rubens created thirty-nine ceiling paintings, tragically destroyed when the church was struck by lightning in 1718. A veil of subdued awe still hung over the square. I could barely contain my delight: what a joy to be reunited with Rubens in this magical city where he lived and worked—to see the same buildings, walk the same streets, and breathe the same air.

SINT-JACOBSKERK

Next, I paid a visit to the place where Rubens was buried. The seventeenth-century Sint-Jacobskerk (St James's Church), where Rubens lies in the vault under the chapel, adorned with one of his magnificent paintings, would be one of the focal points of my visit. Because of restoration work, it was open only during the summer and only for a few days a week. It was a glorious summer day, the sky a Mediterranean blue, when I entered the dark Gothic church. I was alone and emotionally charged, and the whole day had already felt like a pilgrimage. I stopped in front of the black iron bars that separated the chapel from the main church. The chapel gate was wide open, but I hesitated at the railings. I was stunned by the sight of a black sarcophagus at the top of the steps, as well as by the lightness and joyfulness of the *Our Lady with the Saints*—painted by Rubens himself—above the tomb **[28]**.

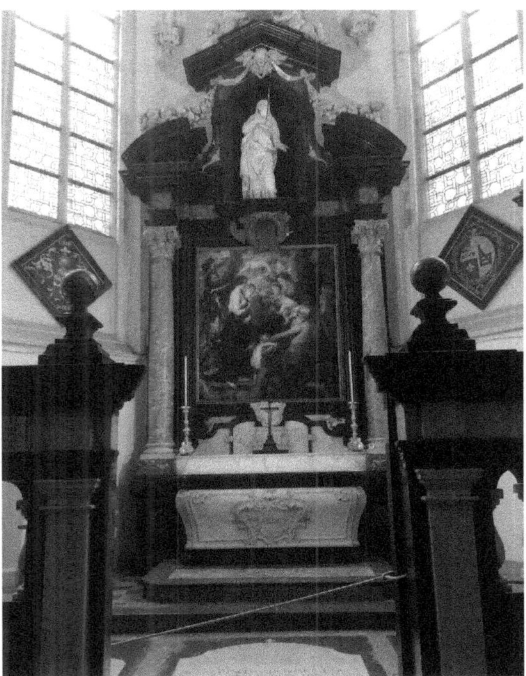

28. Peter Paul Rubens Rubens's tomb in Saint Jacobs, Antwerp.

I suddenly began to weep with huge sobs which echoed through the church. My body was doing something I was not in control of. I was so suprised by this outburst of sobs that my mind was racing to try and figure out what was happening to me. There were rivers of tears, and I had no handkerchief. I began wiping my streaming nose on my shirt cuffs and stood transfixed, in a state of bewilderment. What was strange was that I did not feel sad or even melancholy about Rubens; after all, as I told myself, he had died more than 350 years ago. "For all I know, he may have been a relative of mine", I thought for a second.

I stood there for about twenty minutes crying streams of tears. Then I went out into the sunshine and, as I walked out the door, the sobbing and the weeping stopped immediately. I tidied myself up a bit and went to meet a friend at the coffee shop on the corner. I told him what had happened, and he commented that I was maybe exhausted from the last few months in London.

    BLOOD IS THICKER THAN WATER

The next day I continued my Rubens pilgrimage by visiting his home. The house where Rubens lived and worked for most of his life is located on the Wapper, just off the Meir, a pedestrian boulevard linking the nineteenth-century city with the old town. Once home to Antwerp's aristocrats (including the first Belgian kings), the Meir now hosts every major European chain store. After negotiating the hustle of Saturday morning shoppers 'doing the Meir', entering Rubens's courtyard was like stepping back into the seventeenth century. His contemporary, Jan van de Wouwer, had predicted that Rubens's spectacular residence would "arouse the astonishment of foreigners and the admiration of travellers"[4], and this still holds true today. After several years of intensive restoration, the Rubenshuis opened to the public on the national day of Belgium, 21 July 1946—the year I was born.

Rubens purchased these premises in November 1610, soon after his marriage to Isabella Brandt, but they did not move in until ambitious renovations were completed in 1615. As Rubens's commissions multiplied, so did his wealth, and he spent more and more of his fortune decorating his home. In a letter written on 12 May 1618, to Dudley Carleton, the British ambassador to The Hague, Rubens notes:

> In the past year I have spent several thousand guilders on my house and I would not like to exceed the limits of my budget just in order to please a fancy. All in all I am no prince, but someone who has to live off the fruits of his labor.[5]

Evidently, Rubens was a shrewd negotiator. He had just purchased from Carleton some ninety ancient sculptures intended for the grand marble gallery that he had custom-built.

The courtyard was like a Renaissance stage set, with its theatrical portico linking the traditional sixteenth-century house on the left with the baroque wing that Rubens designed and built as his studio. The external wall of his studio is a showpiece in itself—a gallery of mischievous satyrs, ancient philosophers, and marble gods. Crowning the portico are two bronze statues of Hermes and Athena by Eduard Deckers, symbolising the successful symbiosis of trade and art in this household. Beyond the arched portico lies the garden—all secret nooks and shady bowers, the flowerbeds arranged as daintily as a box of Belgian chocolates. Church bells chimed in the distance and a sleepy little fountain sang flirtatiously. The whole garden oozed romance. When Rubens lived here, the shooting gallery of the Guild of Arquebusiers ran along the back wall of his property. Nowadays, it is bordered by the Rubenianum.

The interior of Rubens's home has all the trappings of a plush seventeenth-century home: golden leather wallpaper, stained-glass cherubs floating in the windows, exquisite cabinets inlaid with pastoral scenes, and a dwarf-size bed draped with velvet and lace. A portrait of an infant on her deathbed serves as a macabre reminder of the untimely deaths of Rubens's first wife and his twelve-year-old daughter, Clara Serena, in this house. In the next room, I found a happier memento: the cracked leather chair inscribed *Pet. Pavl. Rvbens 1633*, commemorating his appointment as Honorary Dean of the Painters' Guild of Saint Luke.

RUBENS'S ART COLLECTION

Rubens's house, which stands in its original location and has been preserved in its original state, holds a wealth of clues about the artist's professional practices. Rubens was a passionate collector of art and antiquities: the inventory of his estate includes over 300 works of art. In the art gallery, a fine selection of Flemish paintings suggests how this collection might have been displayed during Rubens's time. He himself features in *The Art Gallery of Cornelis van der Geest*, a *Kunstkammer* painting by Willem van Haecht dated 1628. Rubens is portrayed as the gracious courtier admiring van der Geest's collection together with Archduke Albert, the Infanta Isabella, Nicolaas Rockox, Prince Wladislaw of Poland, and other distinguished people. Van Haecht exercised his artistic licence in this symbolic gathering: in 1628, the Archduke Albert was already dead, while Prince Wladislaw did not visit the Netherlands until much later.

The gallery also contains several of Rubens's own oil sketches, including the *modello* for *St Clare of Assisi*, one of the ceiling paintings that decorated the Jesuit Church. According to Dr Paul Huvenne, then director of the Rubenshuis:

> From the contract he [Rubens] signed with the heads of order on 29 March 1620, it is yet again clear how much importance was attached to these designs drawn by his own hand, the *modelli*. The paintings themselves…Rubens executed with the assistance of his best pupils including van Dyck.[6]

RUBENS'S STUDIO

As we know, Rubens, very much in the tradition of the artists' studios he had visited in Italy, had an extensive team of collaborators. It is not surprising that his studio is the largest room in the house, for Rubens produced some 2,500 works with the aid of up to one hundred assistants. Not all of them were apprentices: some were fully-fledged masters, like Frans Snyders and Jan Wildens, who were experts in particular genres of painting: portraits, still lives, animals, flowers, or landscapes. Anthony van Dyck, who came to work with Rubens at the age of seventeen, became a master in his own right after a brief apprenticeship. From the mezzanine overlooking the studio, it was easy to imagine Rubens showing off his handiwork to his royal guests and distinguished patrons while dozens of assistants worked conscientiously below. Two excellent studio copies of his portraits of the Archduke Albert and Isabella hang in the antechamber adjoining the studio. As court painter, Rubens undertook all official portraits of the monarchs, which were then copied by his apprentices. Engravings modelled on these copies were widely distributed.

After an acute attack of gout, Rubens died at home on 30 May 1640 at the age of sixty-two. A few short months later, on 12 December, Antwerp lost another important figurehead, Nicolaas Rockox. Driven by the spirit of the Counter-Reformation and humanist principles, both the artist and the statesman had left their indelible imprint on the city.

ROCKOX'S RESIDENCE

The next landmark of Rubens's Antwerp that I visited was Rockox's residence, The Golden Ring, where the original *Samson and Delilah* had hung for thirty-one years. The Rockoxhuis is to be found at number 12 on Keizerstraat, an elegant street lined with the houses of sixteenth- and seventeenth-century merchants, bankers, and politicians. Rockox's next-door neighbour was the celebrated still-life painter Frans Snyders.

Although the latter is equally impressive, Rockox's residence is more stately than Rubens's home—an example of the stylised opulence of the politician compared to the sophisticated understatement of the artist. The Rockoxhuis was converted into a museum between 1972 and 1977 on the initiative of a Belgian bank that had purchased the building in 1970. Rockox was an avid collector of contemporary paintings, classical statuary, and antique coins, and also had an extensive library. In order to recreate his household as accurately as possible, the curators consulted the inventory drawn up by the notary David van der Soppen a week after Rockox's death. Van der Soppen counted 203 volumes and 87 paintings, including works by van Dyck, Snyders, Brueghel, and, of course, Rubens. From among these treasures, he singled out one work: "In the groote saleth: an oil painting on wood, framed, depicting Samson and Delilah, a work by Mr Rubens."[7]

With its row of large windows overlooking a peaceful courtyard, Rockox's great salon was smaller than I had imagined, but the fireplace was larger, taller, and much more imposing. I was stunned by its enormous height, which makes it reminiscent of other contemporary Antwerp fireplaces—many of them now in the Plantin-Moretus Museum. As a chimney-piece painting, *Samson and Delilah* would have made a striking conversation point among the dignitaries that Rockox would have entertained. I imagined the real work hanging there, imposing and atmospheric, as in the Francken *Kunstkammer* painting of the room. There was no way that NG6461 would have been at home there. It just wasn't good enough. Little did I know at the time that, some years later, this same painting from the National Gallery would travel all the way to Antwerp to hang at this very spot.

ROYAL MUSEUM OF FINE ARTS

The following day, after breakfast in the sun-splashed Groenplaats, I took a taxi to the Royal Museum of Fine Arts, a late-nineteenth-century building in the belle époque Het Zuid style. A single visit to this amazing collection is like taking an entire course in the Golden Age of Flemish art. A spectacular marble staircase leads directly into the Rubens Hall. As ever, I was amazed by the ingenious composition, sublime subtlety, and intense sensuality of his huge originals. There were very few visitors, but all the great masters were there. Here were Rubens's Flemish predecessors with their exquisite porcelain women: the haunting translucence of Lucas Cranach's *Adam and Eve*; the alabaster poise of Quentin Massys's *Saint Mary Magdalene*; his son Jan's cool *Judith*, who is holding the severed head of Holofernes like a plaything. And there were Rubens's contemporaries: Frans Snyders's cheeky monkey stealing peaches from a feast of fruit; the intricate bouquets of 'Velvet' Jan Brueghel the Elder; the religious perfection of Maerten de Vos; the immaculate portraits of Anthony van Dyck.

An entire gallery was dedicated to Jacob Jordaens (Antwerp, 1593–1678), one of Rubens's most talented and idiosyncratic students. I paused in front of his *Meleager and Atalanta*. The dramatic handling of light and the figure in red gesturing towards the young couple are straight out of Caravaggio. Meleager and Atalanta are exceptionally well painted, but display a coarse lack of idealisation that would have been as shocking in Jordaens's day as it is today. One of the contenders for the authorship of NG6461 is, according to some critics, Jordaens[8]. In my opinion, Jordaens was far too talented a painter to have produced such early-twentieth-century neo-impressionistic, slapdash work. Visually, Jordaens was eccentric: his distorted forms verge on the grotesque. However, the fact that he was attracted to weird forms (disfigured turkeys and unpleasant parrots, female nudes with awkward features and discordant proportions) does not detract from the fact that he was one of Rubens's star pupils, capable of carrying off any subject with amazing skill.

As I strolled through the galleries, I became aware that local artists had been making monumental altarpieces for several generations before Rubens. I was enormously impressed by Frans Floris (Antwerp, 1519/20–70), an excellent draughtsman who combines an awareness of Italian art with the neatness and perfection of execution of Flanders. His monumental *Fall of the Rebel Angels* is, surely, one of the most ambitious compositions ever painted: a ferocious battle between the good angels and their fallen siblings, who have morphed into boar-headed devils, dragons, and other monstrous creatures. The precision with which this hellish scene is rendered brings to mind Hieronymus Bosch, who worked on a smaller scale, and casts a whole new light on twentieth-century surrealism.

Rubens was very specific about which of his assistants were authorised to make legitimate copies of his work. A flawless copy of Rubens's *The Descent from the Cross*, painted by an anonymous apprentice from his studio, left no doubt in my mind about the consummate skill of the chosen few. No modern copyist could be so assured. During my visit to the Royal Museum, through the glass wall, I could watch the Museum restorers quietly retouching a couple of Old Masters. I observed them at work, appalled by the notion that a sneeze, an itch, or a momentary loss of muscular coordination could cause the wrist to wobble, the brush to slip, and destroy forever a priceless work of art.

This was my cue to head for the Cathedral of Our Lady to admire Rubens's celebrated altarpieces[9] in the flesh, so to speak.

Above the gigantic altar, Christ hung crucified in mid-air. On either side were Rubens's tremendous triptychs. On the left was *The Elevation of the Cross* **[29]**, the surging struggle to hoist Christ onto the Cross, his pale body angling diagonally skywards, testing the strength of the Cross-bearers, the latter flushed with exertion, their toes tensed. On the right was *The Descent from the Cross* **[30]**,

29. Peter Paul Rubens
The Elevation of the Cross

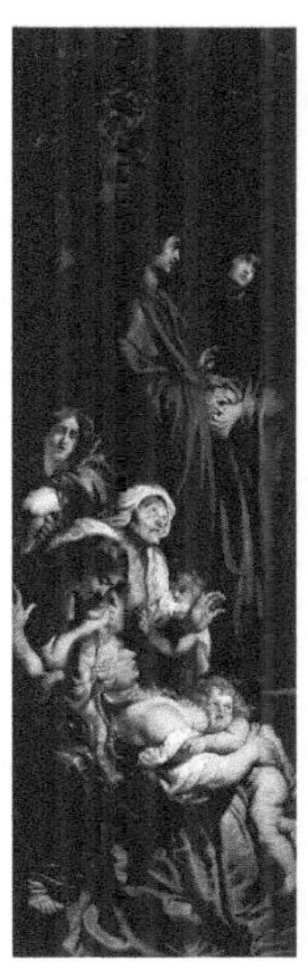
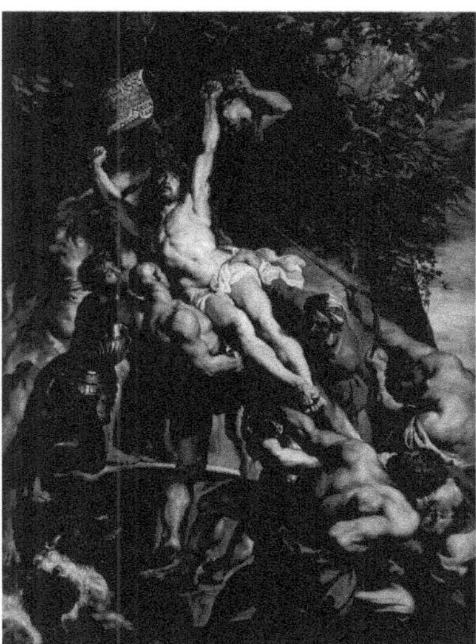
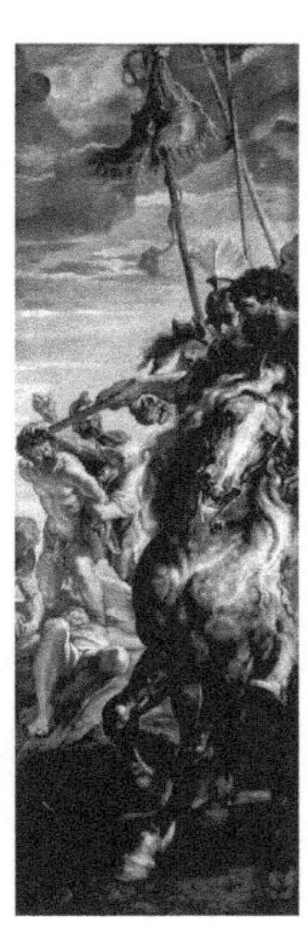

30. Peter Paul Rubens
The Descent from the Cross

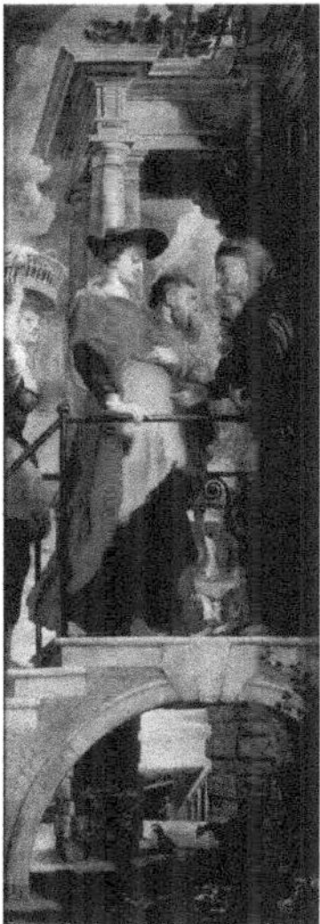
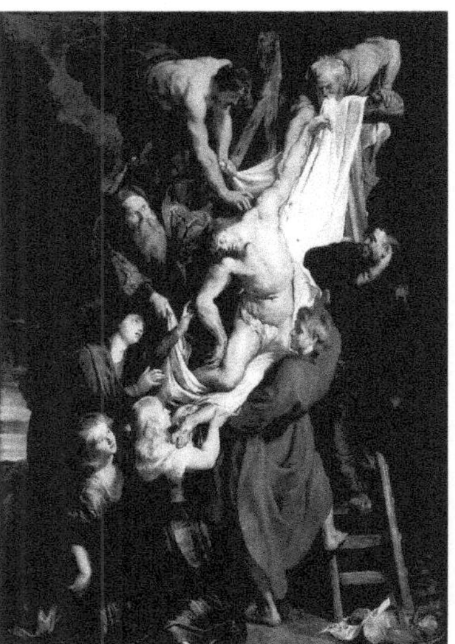
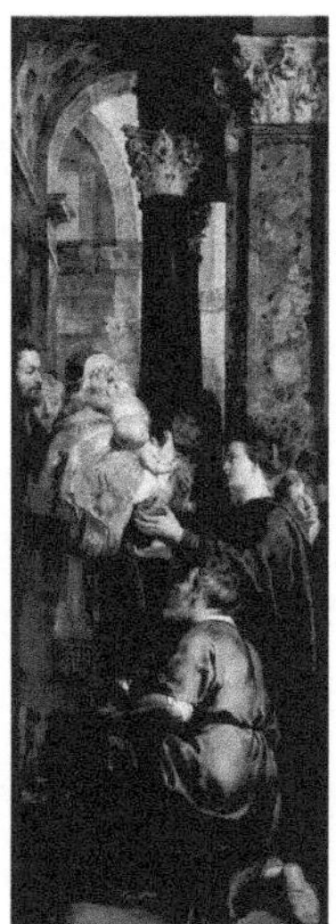

the drooping figure of Christ as he is lifted down, limp and broken, by a circle of mournful followers. In this cold and cavernous space, the sensuality of Rubens's figures—their all-too-human flesh, their emotional turmoil—was accentuated.

THE ELEVATION OF THE CROSS

Seeing *The Elevation of the Cross* for the first time took my breath away. Towering over me—4.6-metres tall and three-panels wide—my first impression was that it had been created by some superhuman power. I suddenly understood why, in this cathedral, in this city, and among connoisseurs the world over, Rubens is hailed as a god of painting. I sat down in one of the pews and feasted my eyes. Although I did not intend to take any photographs so as not to disturb the mid-morning mass that was in progress, I took out my telescopic lens to examine those details that are invisible to the naked eye because of the sheer scale of the work. Through the lens the paint became tactile, creating the illusion that I could actually feel the gestures that had made these marvellous brushstrokes on the smooth oak panels.

There was something about the figures in the left-hand panel that seemed strangely familiar. My gaze lingered on the young woman in red with her cascades of thick, blonde hair, her breasts exposed, and her body tilted backwards. She seems taken aback by the violence of the crucifixion she is witnessing. Created by a whirlwind of inspired brushstrokes, this young woman has a very real presence. Her golden locks have a sculptural texture thanks to the extraordinary richness of the impasto. Her delicate complexion is handled with the same sensuality: her flushed cheeks are painted in the characteristic emulsion of oil and protein Rubens always used to paint flesh with. Her illuminated breast is smooth as ivory, but for the subtle green veins scarcely visible through her luminous skin. I smiled, recalling the black streaks that passed for veins on the National Gallery Delilah's pasty breasts [31].

'DELILAH'

Then it struck me: everything about the iconography of this woman (her garments, her facial features, and her hair) were strikingly similar to the National Gallery's Delilah [32, 33]. The two women might have been painted from the same model. They are even wearing the same red dress. But there was one vital difference: the girl before me was a masterpiece; Delilah was not.

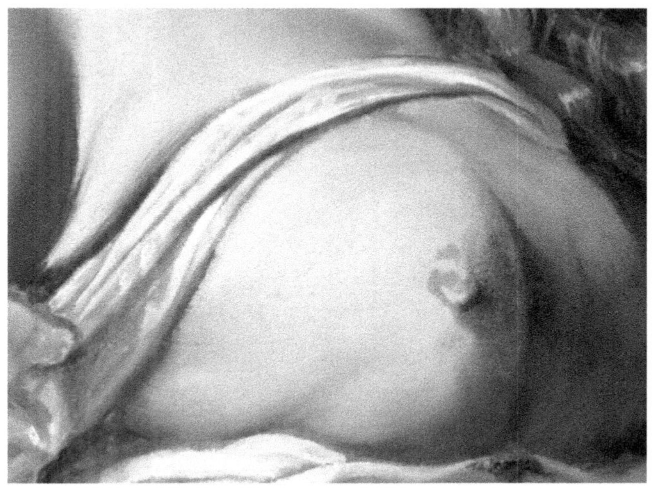

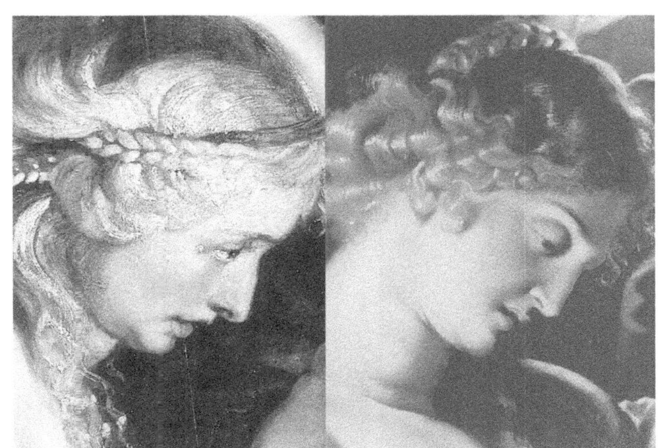

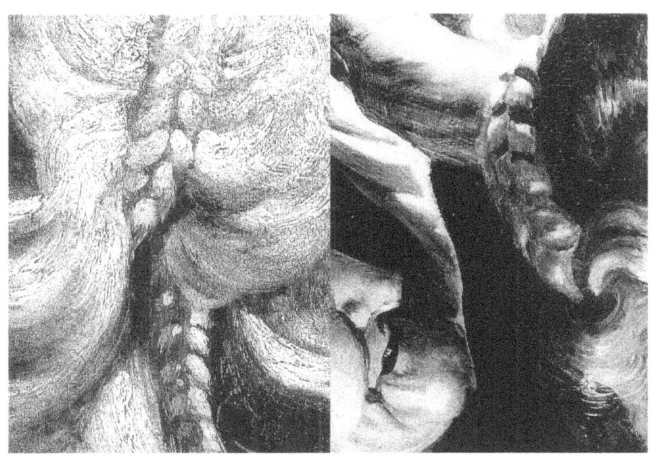

BLOOD IS THICKER THAN WATER

Delilah's hair—though arguably the most convincing detail in the whole picture—pales into insignificance compared with this animated golden mane tumbling over bare shoulders. Unlike the patchy background visible through Delilah's blouse, this woman's white chemise has been painted with very thick impasto, with no gaps in the continuity of the brushstrokes.

OLD CRONE

I then realised that there was not just one familiar figure, but two: the old crone behind the woman in red bore a striking resemblance to the hag leaning over Delilah—a cruel reminder of the transience of beauty and youth [34]. But for all their surface similarities, there was, again, one critical disparity: this old woman was

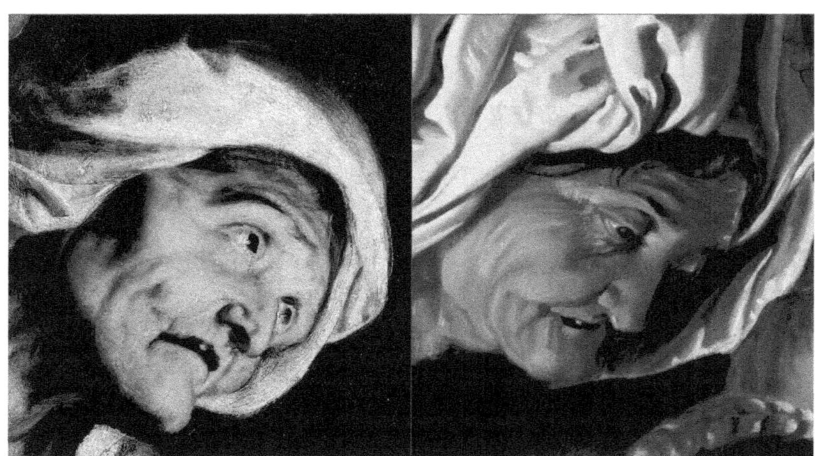

34. Comparison: The old crone in Peter Paul Rubens, *Raising of the Cross* (left); and in NG6461 (right).

painted in a style consistent with Rubens's technique, while the one in NG6461 was in a pseudo-impressionist style popular at the turn of the twentieth century. Her sallow skin, rendered with greenish yellow, middle-tone shadows, has a deathly pallor. Her white headdress is shaded with a subtle, pale grey, in contrast to the brutal handling of her counterpart in NG6461.

MUSCULAR MEN

I turned, again, to the central panel in search of further evidence of cheap imitation. Four of the men raising the cross are stripped to the waist; like Samson, their gigantic proportions owe much to Michelangelo. But here the anatomy works: the feeling of strength is a reality. Their muscular backs, arms, and legs represent the unstoppable force of evil. Recalling Samson's amputated toes,

I looked down at their feet. I counted an astonishing eleven feet in the central panel alone, each one brilliantly executed down to the last toenail. Rubens had used a strong vermilion to show the pressure of the weight of the cross on their feet.

Potent and gutsy, the painting before me pulsated with life. Although NG6461 contained almost identical iconographic elements, it was no more than a ghostly imitation of this magnificent original. When I subsequently compared the restoration reports, I was shocked by the differences in colours. *The Elevation of the Cross*, painted only one year after *Samson and Delilah*, contains a whole spectrum of precious colours, including about seven different shades of blue, whereas NG6461 does not contain a single blue!

I was further amused by an oddly playful detail in the triptych: the dog in the bottom left of the central panel. It is not the mongrel one would expect to find yapping at the heels of the crucifiers, but a fluffy pedigree who would be more at home in a royal court. I later discovered a reasonable explanation for this odd anachronism. The dog was not part of the original composition; Rubens added it at a later date, because the presumptuous priests of St Walburga, who commissioned the work, had complained that the gap in the corner was too big for their liking.

DESCENT FROM THE CROSS

The funereal *Descent from the Cross* reveals a more 'mature' Rubens who, only two years later, had shrugged off the youthful theatricality expressed in *The Elevation*. *The Descent* was commissioned in 1611 by the Guild of Arquebusiers, whose patron saint was St Christopher, the bearer of Christ. As a tribute to his patrons, Rubens subtly transforms every figure in the triptych into a bearer of Christ. In the central panel, eight mourners extend their arms towards the corpse of Christ, the bright red cloak of John contrasting with his lifeless body. On the left, the Virgin bears Christ in her belly; behind her is Elizabeth, soon to give birth to John the Baptist. On the right, Simeon holds the baby Jesus in his arms, while Mary 'supports' the infant with her upturned hands. Behind Simeon, a gentle onlooker watches the scene with a tender smile; he is none other than Nicolaas Rockox, Dean of the Guild of Arquebusiers, who commissioned this altarpiece from his friend Peter Paul.

I have always felt a very powerful sense of loss and mourning present in *The Descent*. For many years, a black-and-white engraving of the painting hung in the Church of St Theodore in the First Cemetery in Athens. As a young girl, I remember fixing my gaze on it to avoid looking at my grandfather's body lying in state. Later in my life, other beloved dead passed from that church; their deaths were all present in that engraving of Rubens's *The Descent from the Cross*. When the church was renovated, Orthodox purists decided to remove this icon of Western Catholicism. How strange to find it again in this grandiose cathedral so far from home.

The two altarpieces were so stunning that I felt recharged with spirituality and beauty. I backed out of the church, feeling I could take on the world. The oak angels and saints watched me go—a monochrome vision of dark brown, as if to help me retain the joyous polychromy of Rubens.

ISABELLA OF BOURBON

Near the exit I stumbled on what looked like a granite table. It was a bronze statue of a lady wearing a crown, her hands joined together in prayer. She looked so serene, lying there with her two little dogs curled up at her feet. I wondered who she could be. An old gentleman stepped out of the shadows to answer my silent query.

"She is Isabella of Bourbon, our bronze lady. Late fifteenth century. The work of an anonymous sculptor from Brussels".

My old guide peered at Isabella through his round, horn-rimmed glasses.

"She was the second wife of Charles the Bold. She used to be in the Abbey of Saint Michael. When the abbey was sold, she was moved here".

I bent down to get a closer look at Isabella. Her face was scarred with jagged gashes.

"The iconoclasts", explained my guide. "They smashed the sarcophagus in 1566. All that remained was this lid with the effigy. She was surrounded by twenty-four bronze *pleurants* (mourners) who cried for her day and night, but they were stolen. I believe they are now in the Rijksmuseum in Amsterdam".

Our time was up. Reluctantly, I bid farewell to this incarnation of my grandfather, and to the city of Rubens.

Three months later, at the end of August, the fax machine in my Athens home began whirring. A gift of thirty pages emerged in a continuous roll, with exciting news from the Belgian genealogist Jan Caluwaerts, whom I had commissioned to research the origins of my mother's family before my visit to Rubens's birthplace. The Scheepers family was from Antwerp! Baptism certificates of this Catholic family, marriage certificates, and death notices streamed through in a river of paper. All these events had been registered in the Sint-Jacobskerk, the place where my body had that inexplicable weeping fit. It was the Scheepers, family church, a mere five minutes' walk from their home.

Suddenly, in this fax message, I read that we were Flemish rather than Walloon, and that our ancestors had been traced back to 1750. The brilliant genealogist had found that the Scheepers family had lived on Rozenstraat in Antwerp and then on Paradijsstraat, until their departure for Greece in 1895, never to return.

Jan had lost the trail of the family before 1750 in the Antwerp archives. The family may have come from Aalst, or elsewhere. But until 1750 they were neighbours of the Rubens tomb, neighbours of Nicolaas Rockox's house, and a stone's throw from Rubens's own house on the Wapper. There was more to it than I had originally suspected. The devout Flemish Catholic Scheepers family, a family of engineers and 'geometres', as they called themselves, were in fact immediate relatives of mine.

Thinking back on Antwerp, I remembered that, even before the Sint-Jacobskerk, I had felt I was returning home. My mind went back to that morning in June when I had stood weeping in the church, and I realised that my body had recognised a place which my mind knew nothing about. The main events in my family's life had taken place in the presence of Rubens's grave. He was buried in the vault of the same church as that in which my relatives would have stood every Sunday, and at the most important events in their lives (christenings, weddings, and funerals), for about 150 years.

Matchpoint

The following pages contain telling comparisons, arranged by the celebrated Shalom Shotten who saw the weaknesses of NG6461 already thirty years ago, between well-known—and obviously authentic—works by Peter Paul Rubens on the left page, and NG6461 on the right. They focus on similar themes (heads, hair, hands, draped fabrics, little boys) to better demonstrate the artist's documented skill juxtaposed with the fake painting's slapdash and incopetent execution.

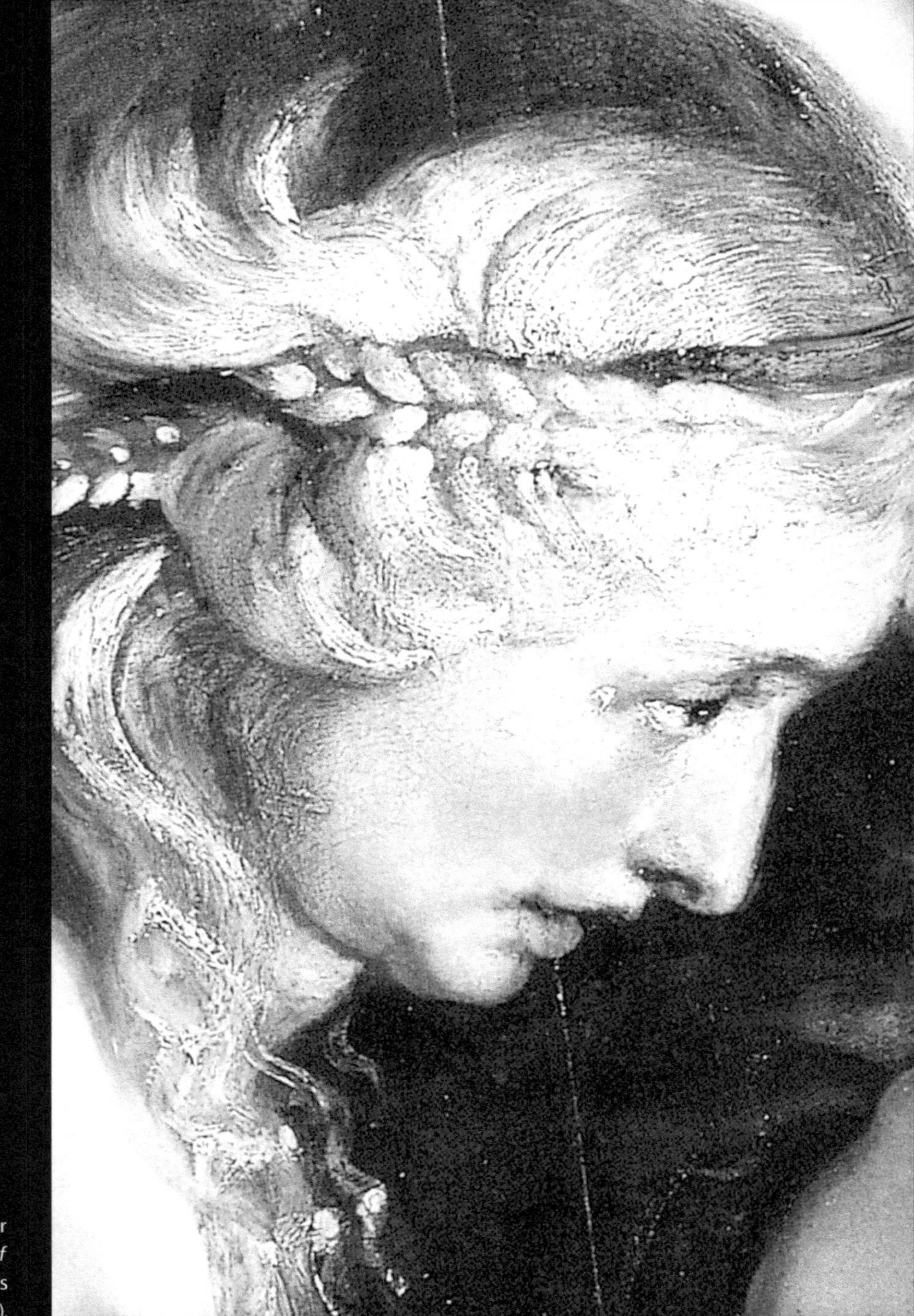

Comparison:
Woman's head in Peter
Paul Rubens, *Raising of
the Cross* (left); Delilah's
head in NG6461 (right).

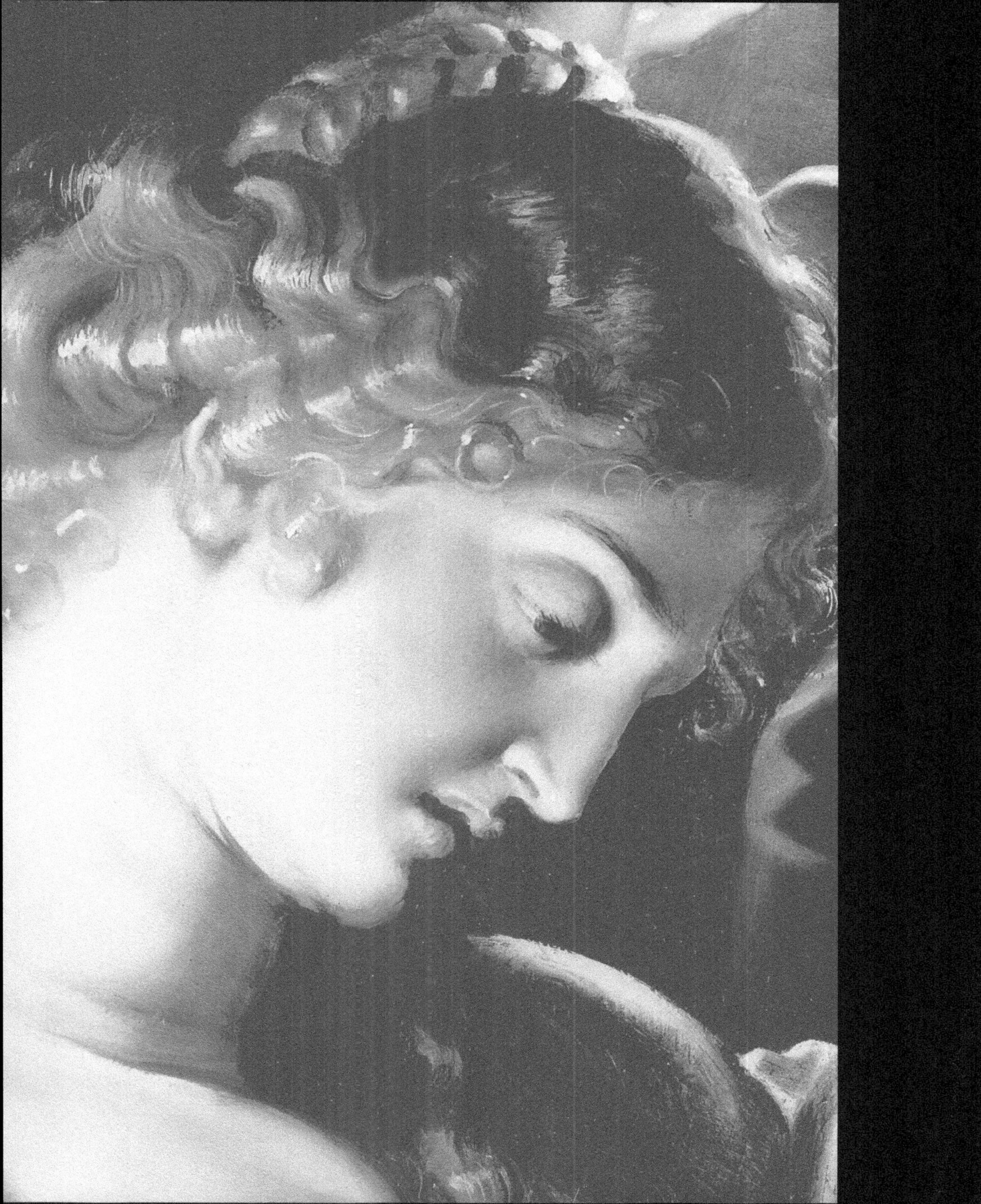

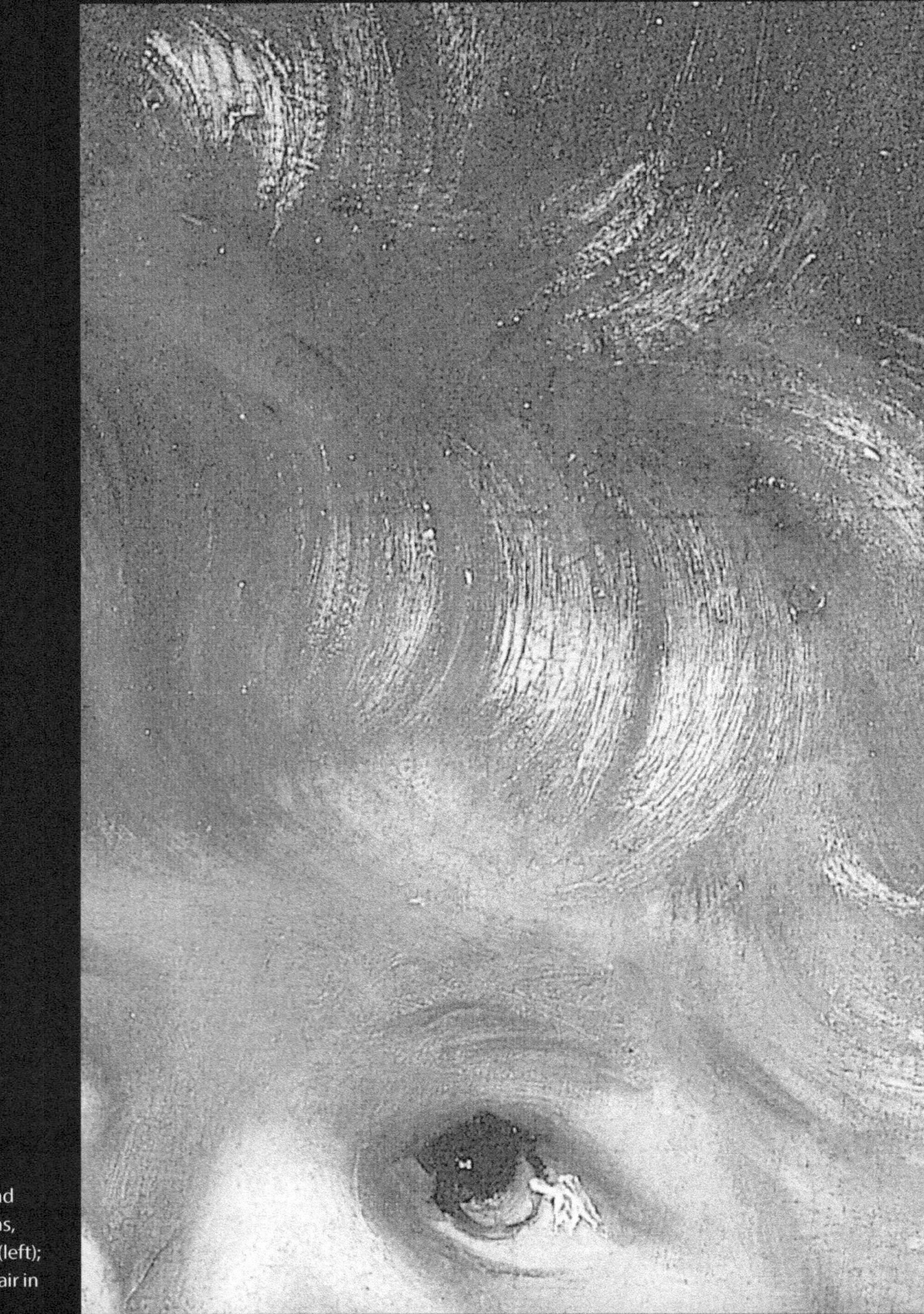

Comparison:
Detail of child's head
in Peter Paul Rubens,
Raising of the Cross (left);
detail of Delilah's hair in
NG6461 (right).

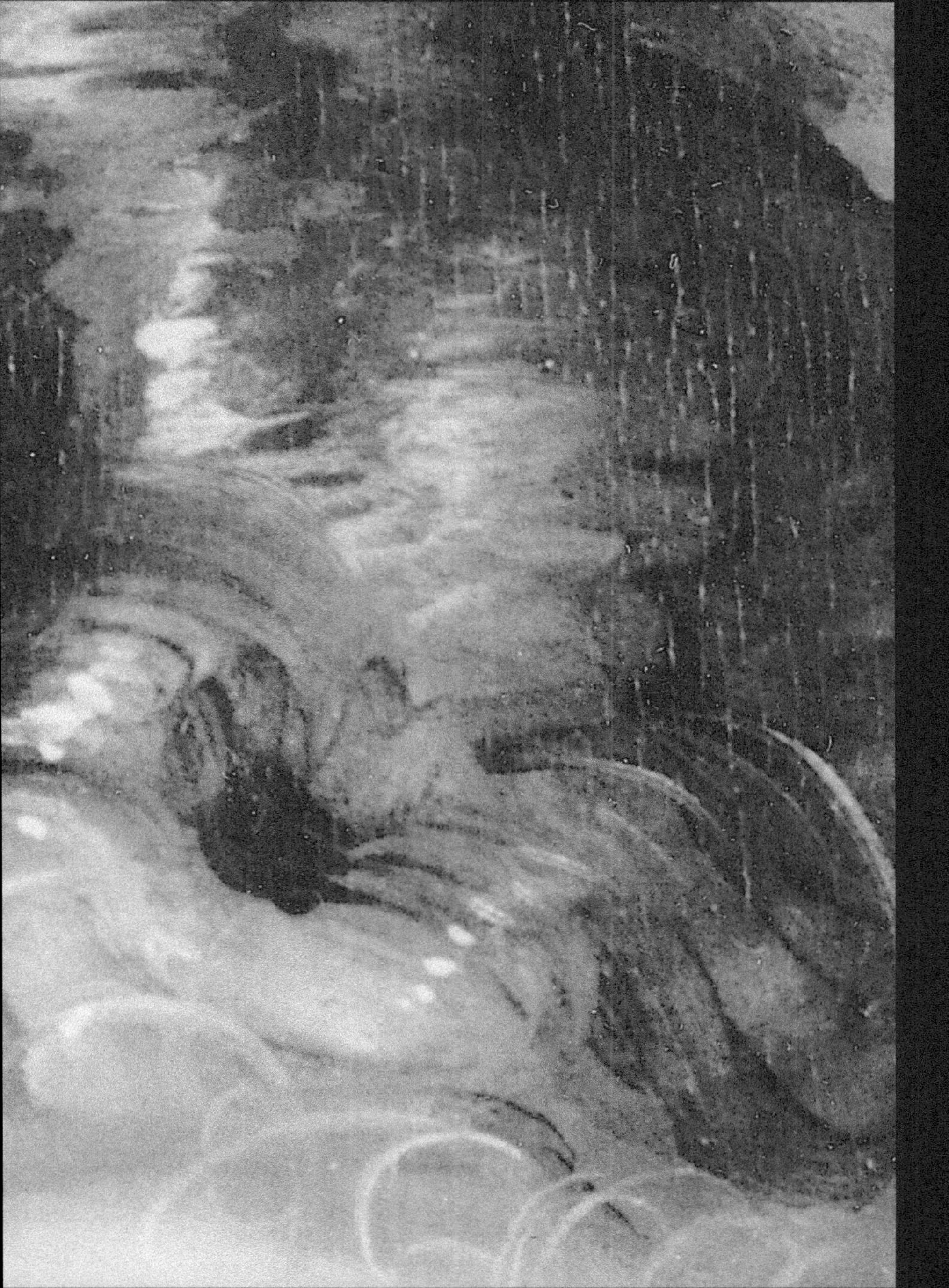

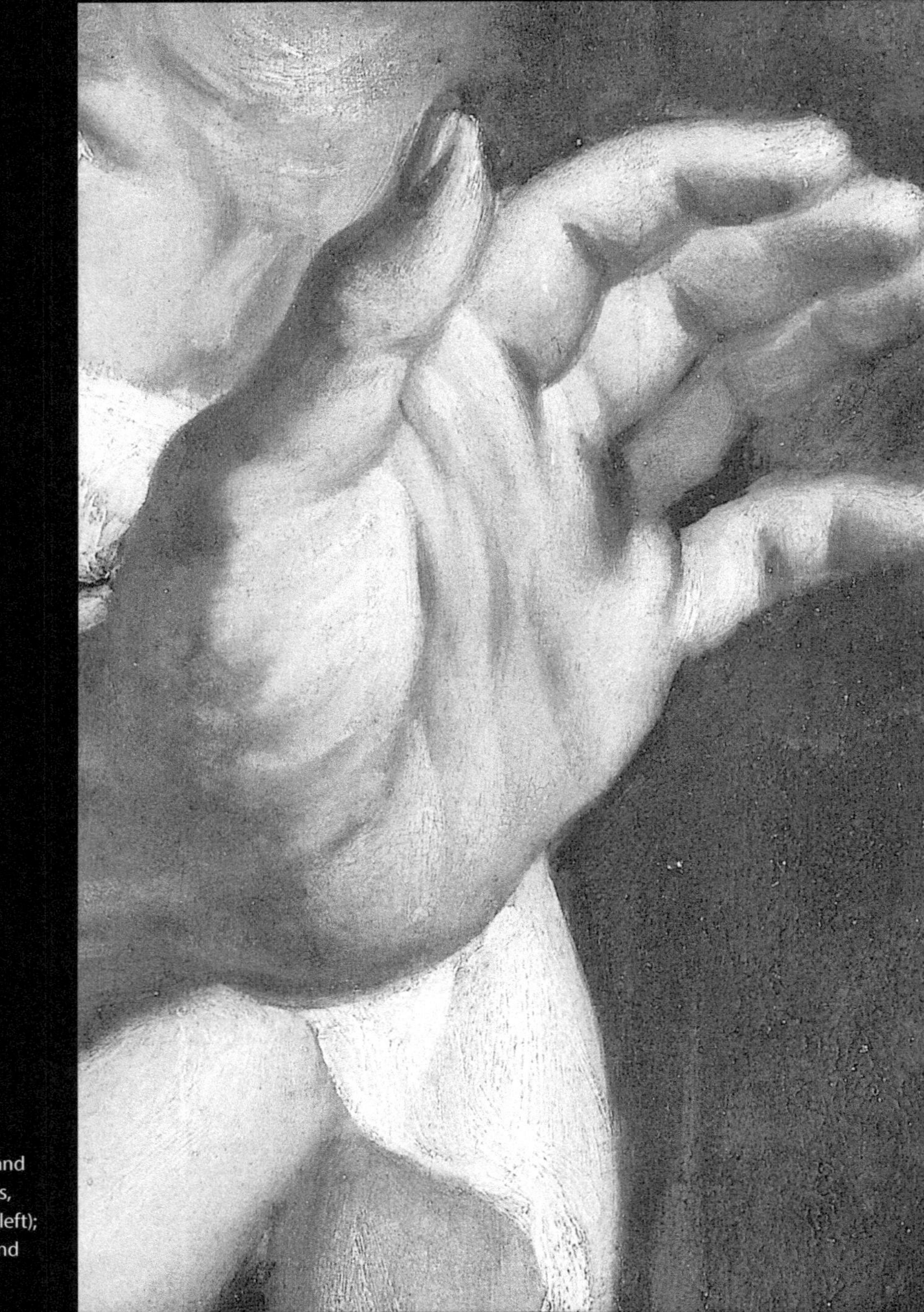

Comparison:
Old woman's left hand
in Peter Paul Rubens,
Raising of the Cross (left);
old crone's right hand
behind the flame in
NG6461 (right).

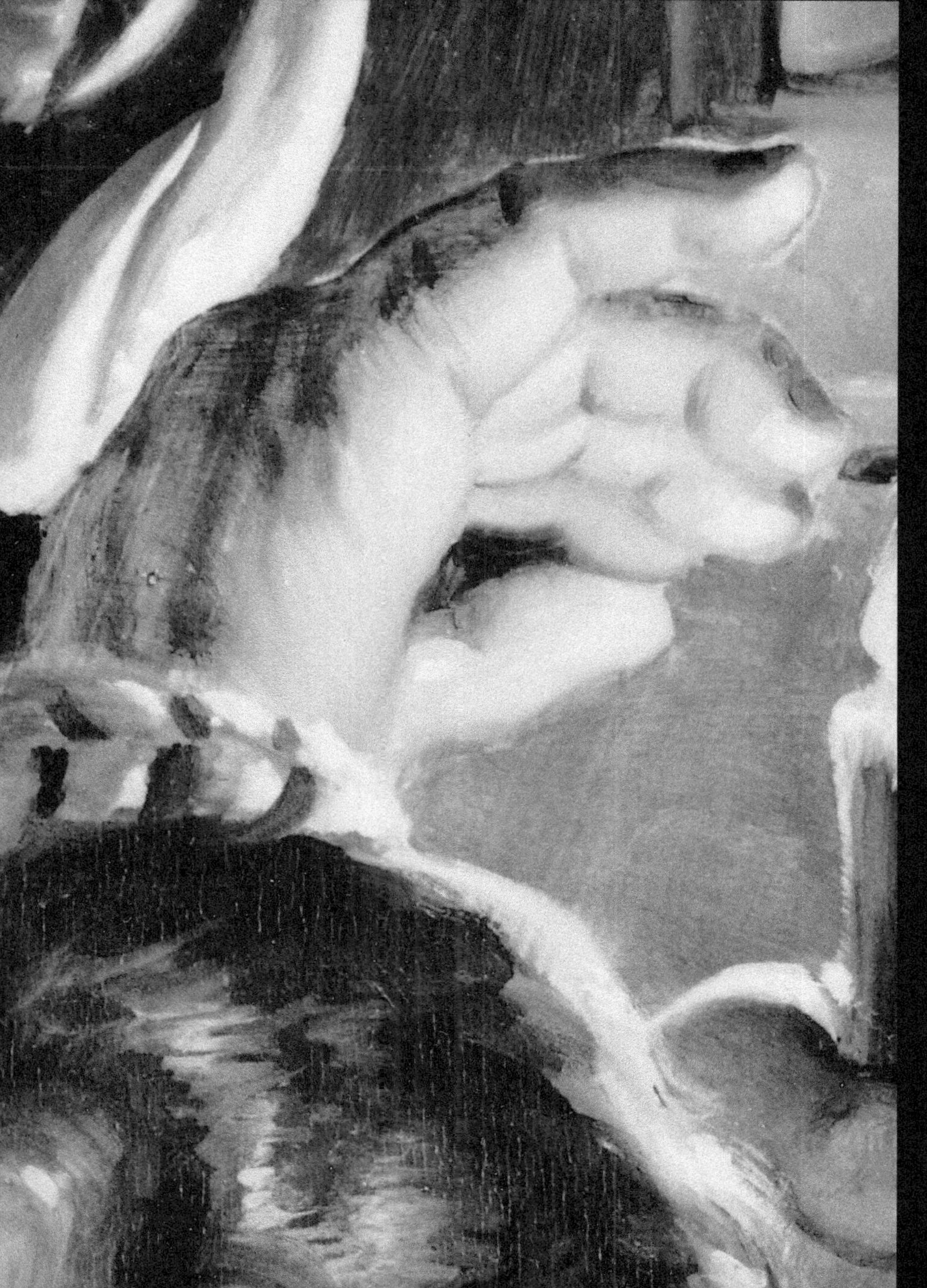

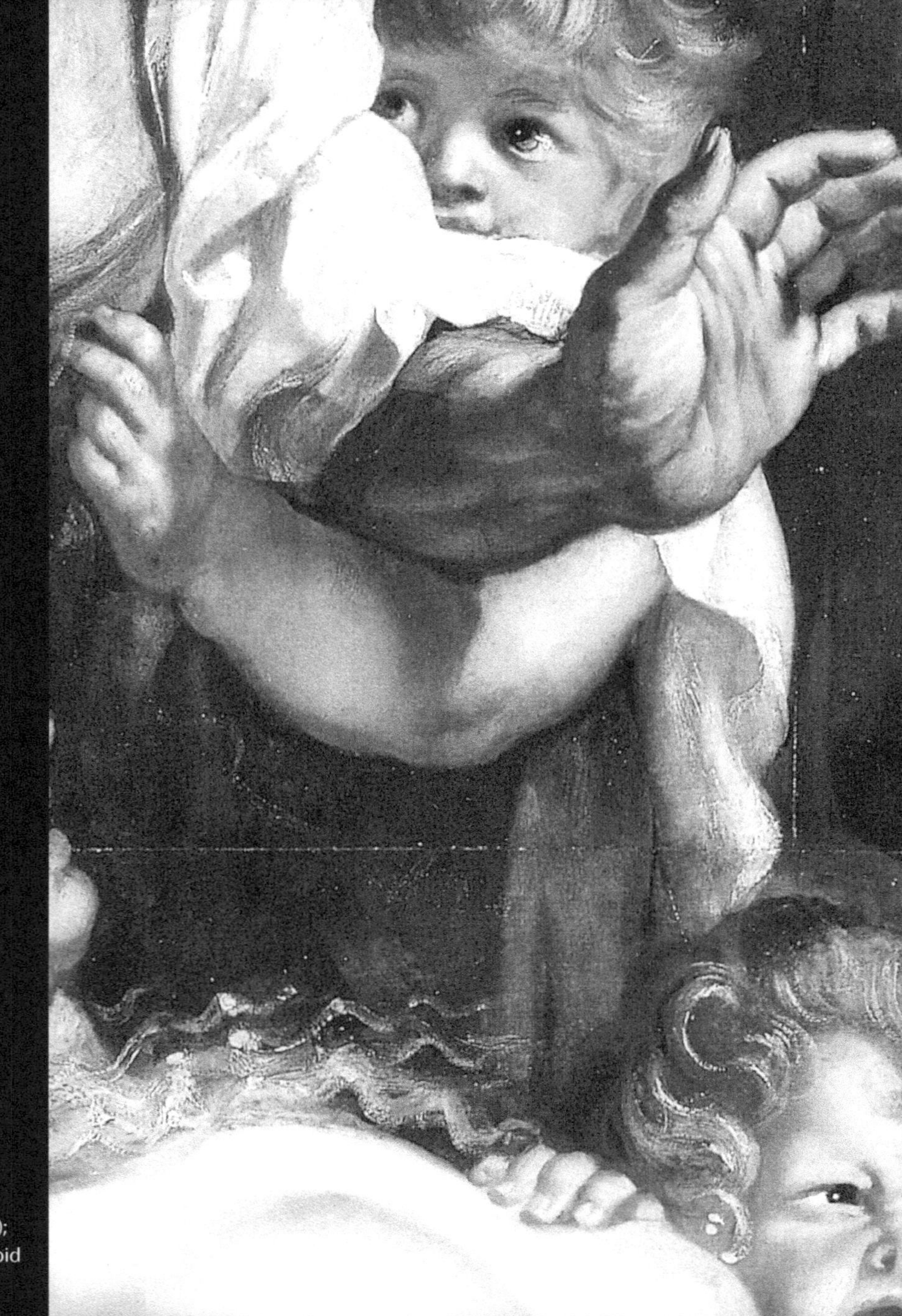

Comparison:
Old woman's left hand
in Peter Paul Rubens,
Raising of the Cross (left);
detail of Venus and Cupid
statuettes in NG6461
(right).

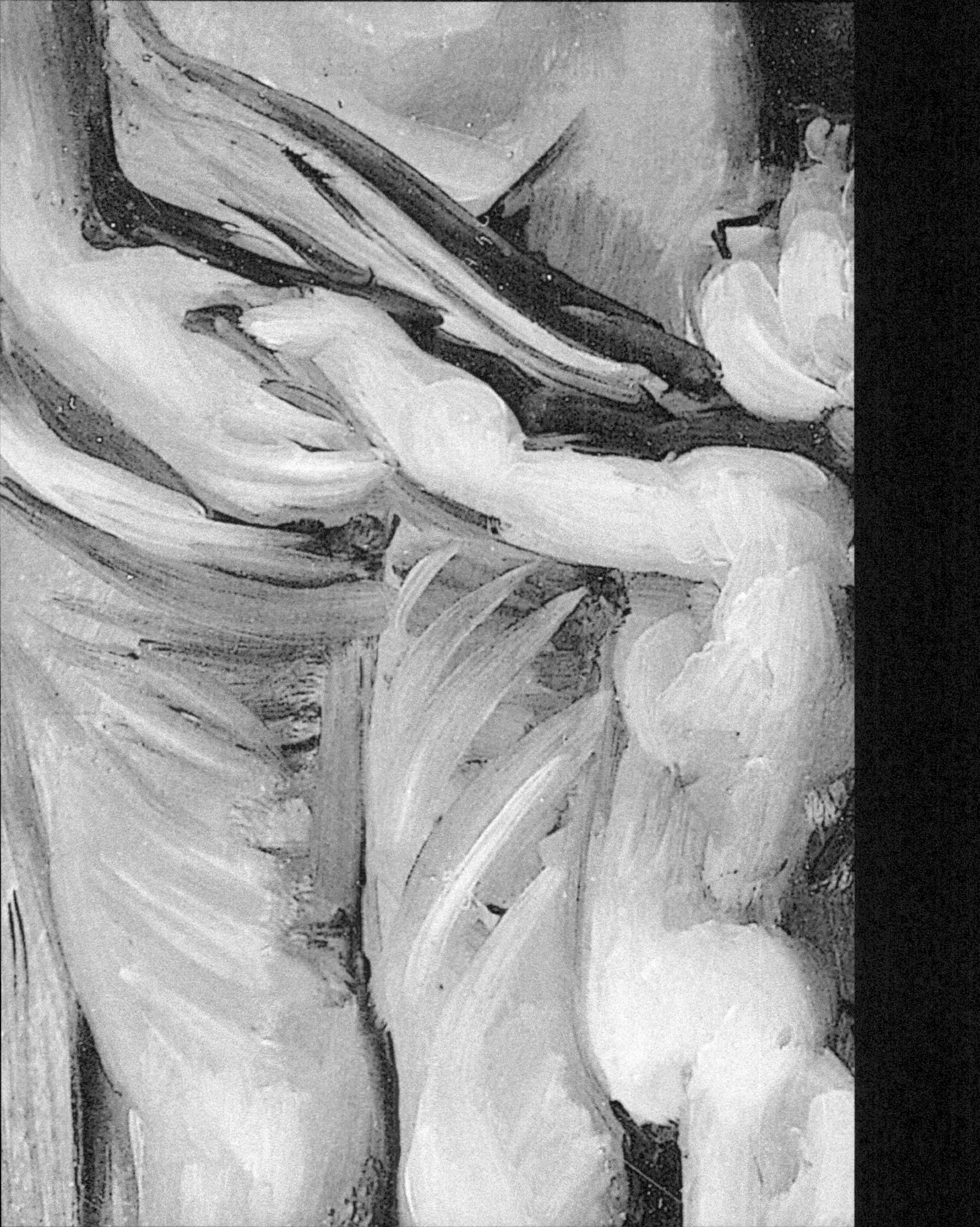

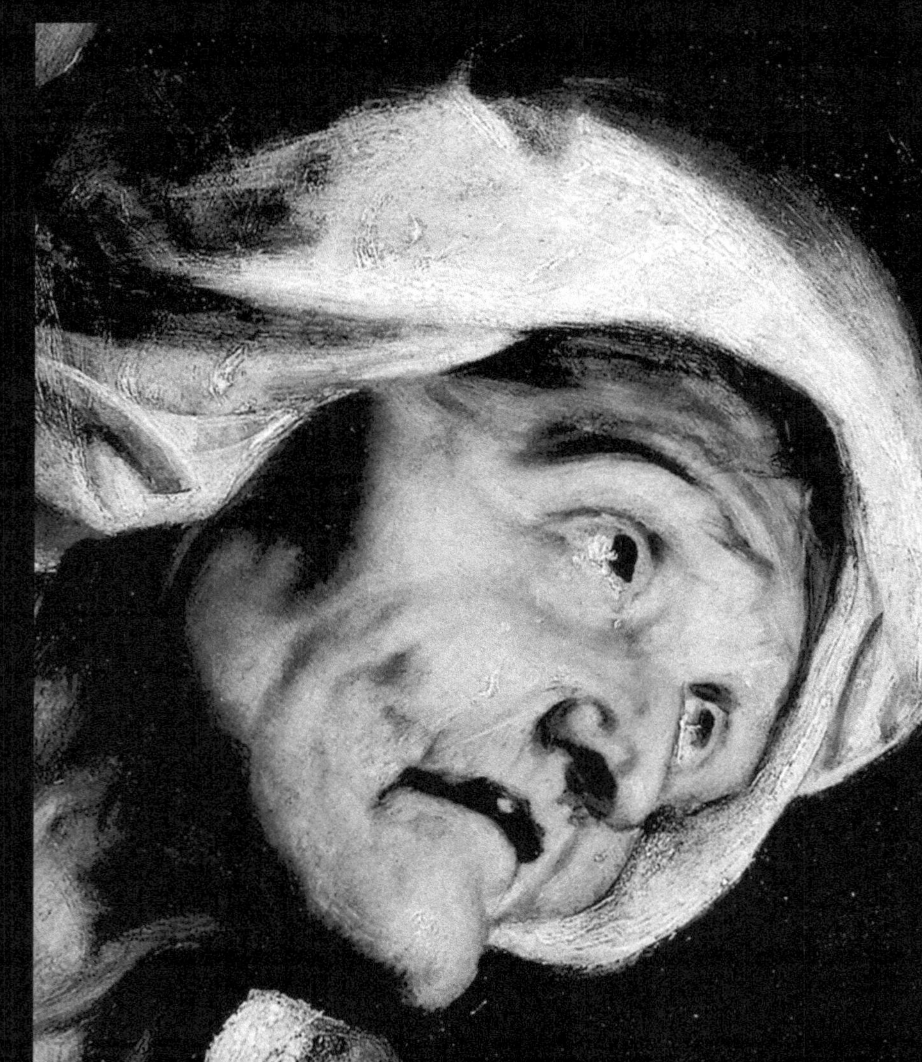

Comparison:
Old woman's head
in Peter Paul Rubens,
Raising of the Cross (left);
old crone's head in
NG6461 (right).

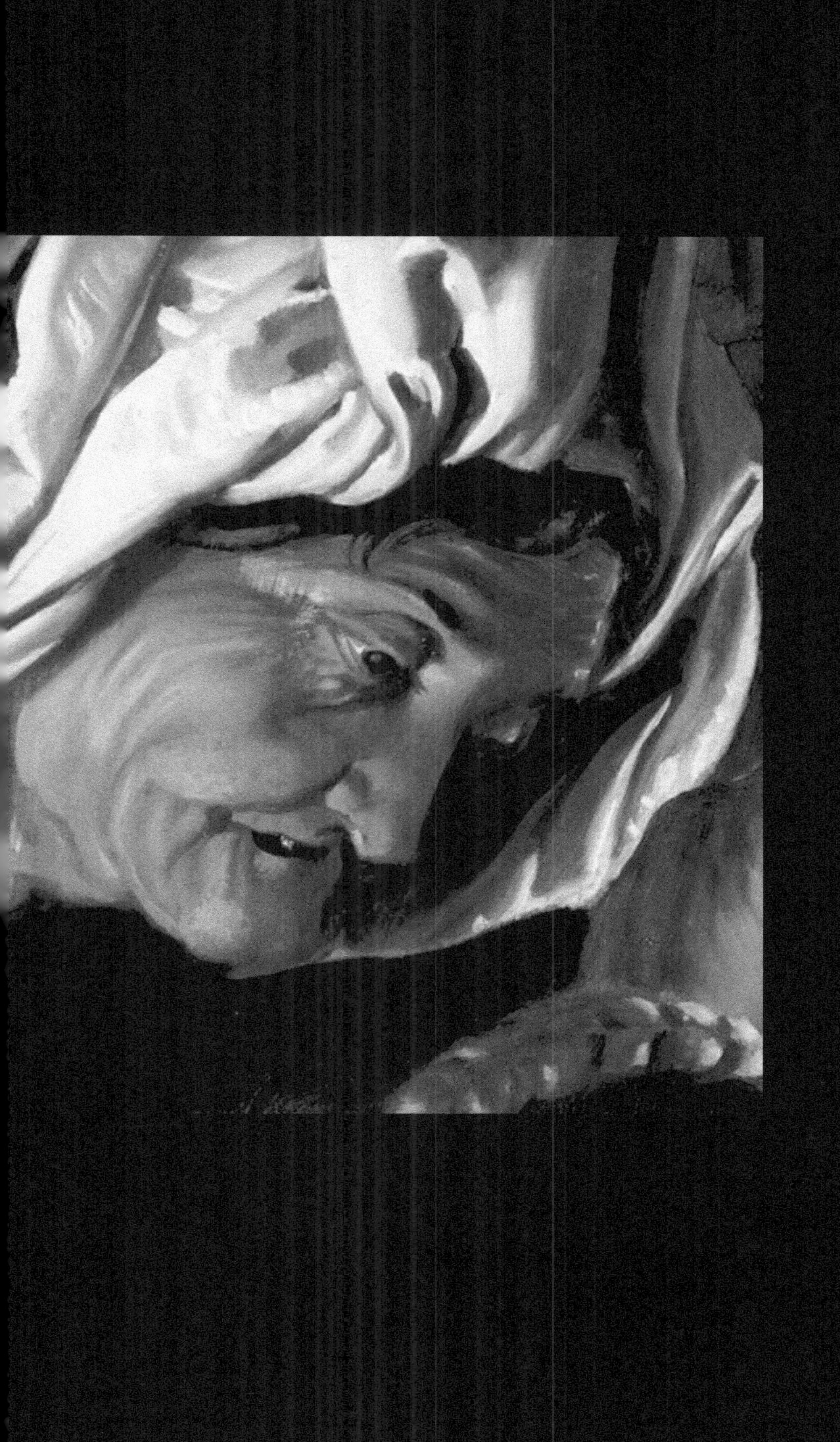

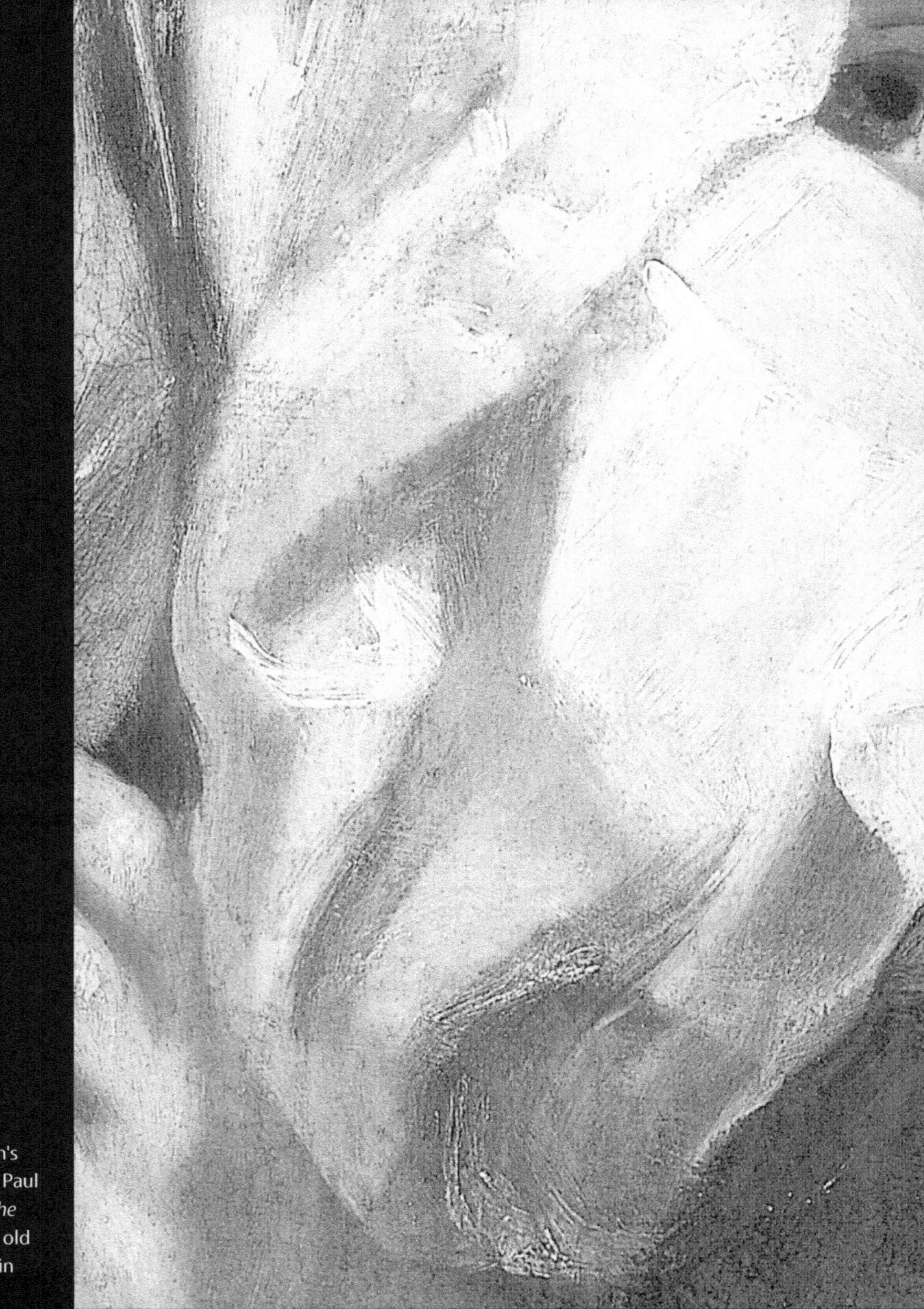

Comparison:
Detail of old woman's head-dress in Peter Paul Rubens, *Raising of the Cross* (left); detail of old crone's head-dress in NG6461 (right).

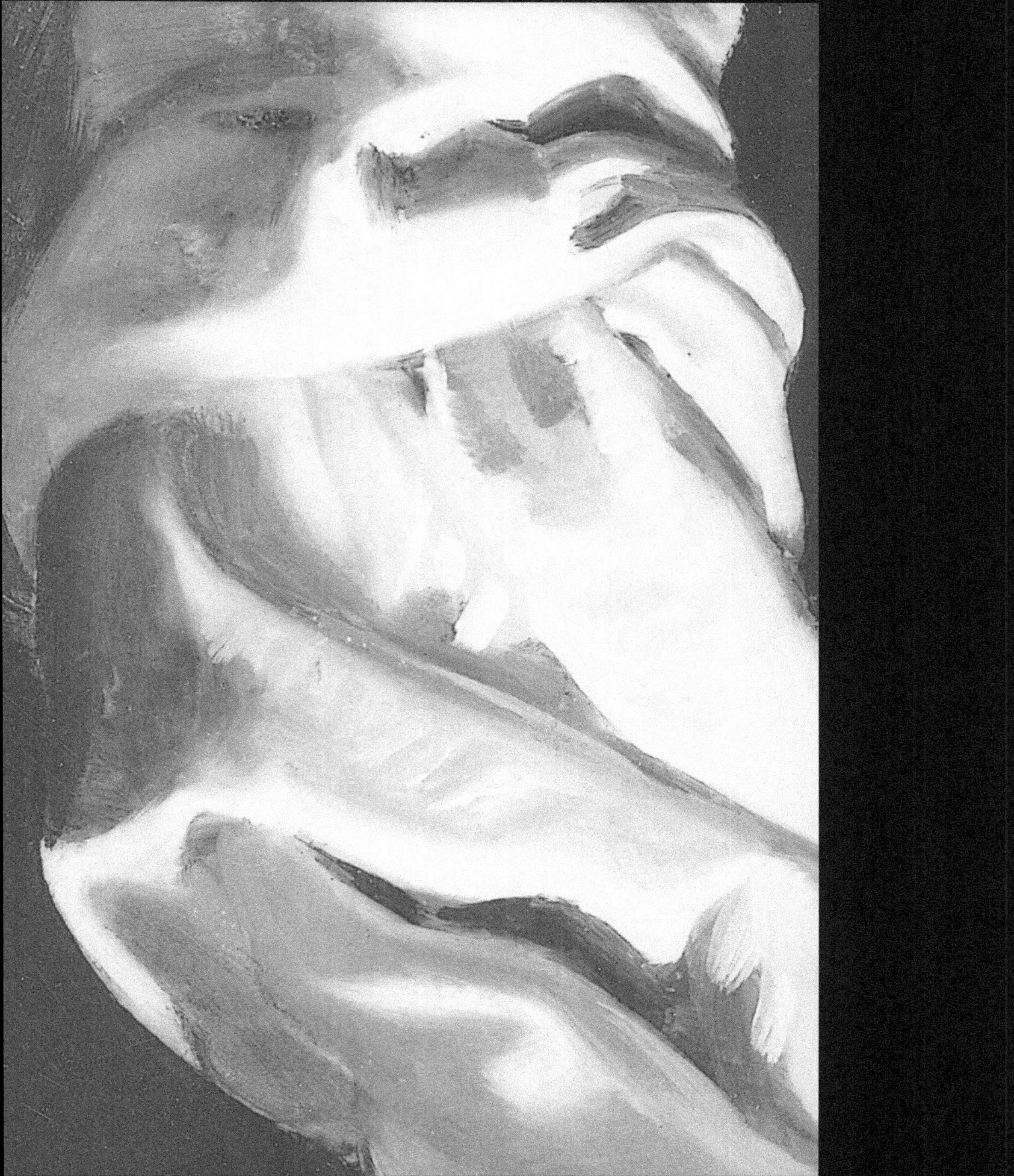

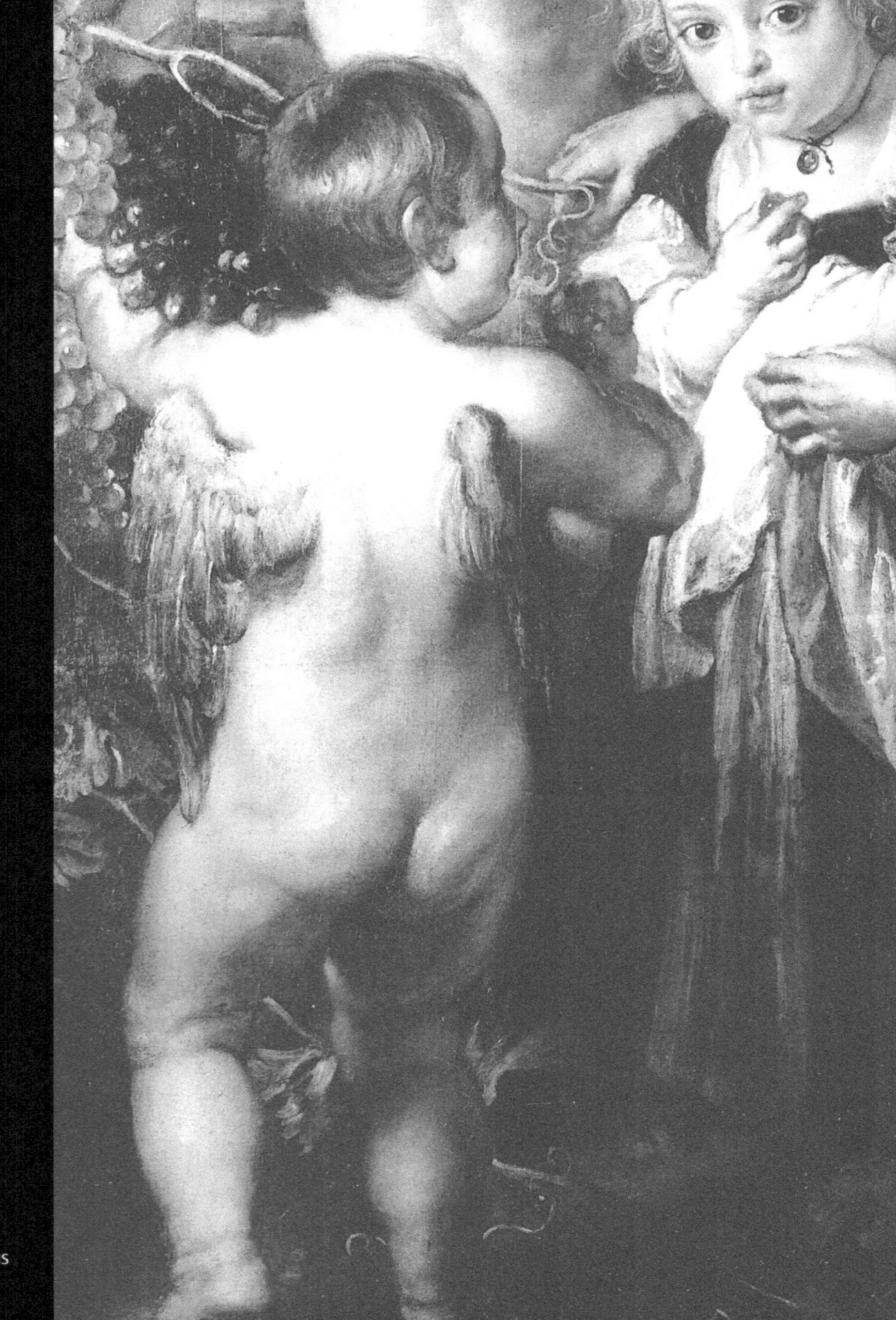

Comparison:
Putto's back in Peter
Paul Rubens, *Peace and
War* (left); detail of Venus
and Cupid statuettes in
NG6461 (right).

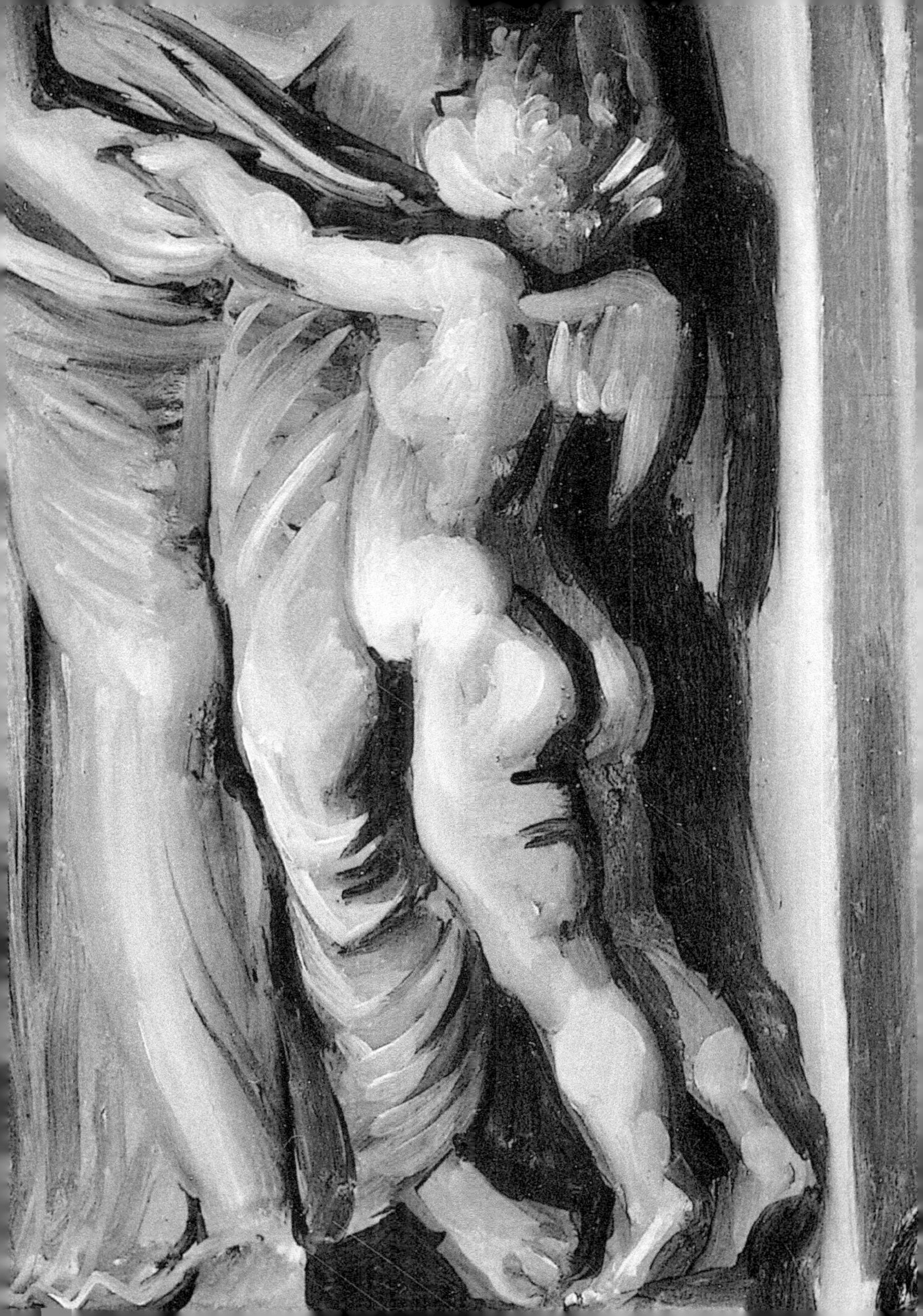

The Keepers of the Keys

FOILED ATTEMPT AT PUBLICITY

In July 1989, the art school broke for summer holidays. I decided to approach a reporter about writing up the Rubens story. I felt that, as a painter, I had exhausted my appetite for academic endeavours. I could see no reason to abandon the work that I loved so much in order to venture into the world of academia, which felt rather stuffy at the time. I was happy with the Pandora's box I had opened, and now it would have to be up to others to write it up and publish it. I felt that the right thing to do was to leave it to professionals, and who better than the arts correspondents of London newspapers? To get an article published in an upmarket scholarly journal, I would have to have ten acronyms after my name. Besides, I thought it would be ideal for a Sunday supplement. So I approached Peter Watson, art reporter at *The Observer*. Watson was intrigued and very enthusiastic about the story. I left with him a large bundle of material, and he promised to run it in the following Sunday's paper.

A few days later I left with my family for Greece, but I kept telephoning Watson from ports and roadside cafes on my way to Corfu. He kept saying: "We might run it this week, or maybe next one". I never heard from Watson again.

This was the beginning of a long period of trying to get the story published and finding the task virtually impossible. Siân, Steve, and I later prepared a report on the problems with NG6461, but I feared that it was not complete or academic enough to send to an art journal like *Burlington* or *Apollo*.

Naturally, I found it extremely frustrating and aggravating that all National Gallery publications from 1989 onwards gave the painting an inordinate amount of publicity. It was featured on the cover of the *Flemish Paintings* booklet written by Christopher Brown for the *National Gallery Schools of Painting* series and hailed as one of the greatest masterpieces of all time. Forgetting for a moment the misunderstandings about its painting techniques that Brown gets himself entangled in, he assures the public that the "*Samson and Delilah* was sold by Rockox's heirs to the Antwerp art dealer Guillaume Forchoudt, who in turn sold it to the prince of Liechtenstein"[1]. But this is plainly unsubstantiated. There is absolutely no evidence for Brown's claim; as we have seen, the painting disappeared after Rockox's death, when it was sold at auction to an unknown buyer in 1641.

The National Gallery has a tradition of accompanying its exhibitions with a catalogue and a dedicated video. NG6461 was included in an exhibition and booklet titled *Director's Choice: Selected Acquisitions 1973–1986*, which marked the retirement of Sir Michael Levey, Director of the National Gallery. Levey waxed lyrical about the painting:

> This masterpiece of Rubens's early maturity shows—one might say shows off—all his abilities as majestic designer and colourist, brilliant, vigorous, and also tender. Looking at these lovers, one is moved to murmur with the Chorus from Milton's *Samson Agonistes* 'Yet beauty, though injurious, hath strange power'.[2]

The idea of Sir Michael murmuring sweet nothings with the Miltonian chorus is quite disconcerting. But this hype was not unusual, and it would continue throughout the coming years. The 1995 exhibition *Frank Auerbach and the National Gallery: Working after the Masters* (19 July–17 September 1995) included NG6461, and the cover illustration for the exhibition catalogue and video was a painting by Auerbach inspired by it.[3] Furthermore, the National Gallery exhibition *Rubens's Landscapes* (16 October 1996–19 January 1997)[4] curiously included NG6461, even though there is no landscape in sight.

In 1991, the painting was featured in yet another special exhibition titled *Brief Encounters*. Van Dyck's *Samson and Delilah* was borrowed from the Dulwich Picture Gallery and the public was invited to make comparisons between the two. This exhibition provoked a very genuine and telling observation by Andrew Graham-Dixon of *The Independent*, who compared Van Dyck's *Samson and Delilah* with NG6461 and the relative merits of the two painters, van Dyck and Rubens, as demonstrated in these paintings. In the one part of the article where the actual handling of paint is discussed, rather than devices such as composition, the reviewer acknowledges that "Van Dyck *outpaints* Rubens, conspicuously, in the depiction of fabrics, rendered here with a liveliness and dash that makes their equivalent in the Rubens seem *ponderous and inert*"[5] [my italics]. Looking at the two paintings, one can only concur.

Mr Graham-Dixon was receptive to the National Gallery's invitation to look at the two paintings with a fresh eye. The result was that he achieved precisely this desired end: he 'saw' only as painters see—without preconceived notions—the shapes and colours which were actually before his eyes. Graham-Dixon perceived the truth that became so very apparent with this exhibition of the two works hanging in the same room, which was quite simply that the van Dyck is a much better painting and that van Dyck *does* outpaint Rubens's ineffective imitator in the rendering of fabrics.

Is it not strange, then, that in the very year in which the *Samson and Delilah* was produced, Rubens also painted a picture that demonstrates his consummate skill in dealing with textures of all kinds? In the self-portrait with his young wife, Isabella Brandt —one of the greatest paintings in Munich's Alte Pinakothek— brocade, silk, velvet, and lace rustle to life in his hands. Rubens's marvellous technical facility and sensitivity to the rhythm of line and colour can be admired here and in countless other of his original paintings throughout the world. Would Graham-Dixon have made the same statement if he had been comparing the *Honeysuckle Bower* in Munich with the Dulwich van Dyck? Van Dyck was a great painter of garments, but he was certainly not more skilful than Rubens. Although he was most probably not aware that this was not a real Rubens, Graham-Dixon could see how bad the textiles and textures of the supposed Rubens painting were.

I could add to Andrew Graham-Dixon's 'fresh' observation that I feel the exhibition helped us confirm our previous suspicion about the two paintings: the student does not outpaint the master; it is, rather, the attribution to the master which must be re-examined. Our original intuition, that the National Gallery picture might not be the original *Samson and Delilah* painted by Rubens for Nicolaas Rockox in 1609, was reinforced by this exhibition.

We wrote to *The Independent* asserting that the reason why Graham-Dixon had rightly noticed these technical flaws was because the National Gallery painting was a copy, and not—as the review claimed—a 'lesser' Rubens. The letter was not published. I suppose everyone to whom this happens feels a sense of grievance, and editors are no doubt wise to avoid cranks. But the way we were so consistently ignored by the press on a matter so publicly debated seemed to us another case of the establishment closing ranks, and yet further proof that those who question recognised authority are all too likely to be dismissed as fools and denied careful consideration of their arguments.

CORRESPONDENCE WITH EDWARD HALL

In 1991 we prepared a detailed sixteen-page report on the issues with NG6461 and decided to send it to several people for their views. I thought it was time to find an independent assessor with scientific knowledge.

Earlier that year I had seen, in an issue of the *Minerva* archaeological magazine, a feature by the retired professor Edward Thomas Hall entitled "Finding the Fakes". Professor Hall, together with Stuart Young, had established the Research Laboratory for Archaeology and the History of Art at the University of Oxford in 1955. We got his address from the magazine and, on 26 October 1991, sent him our report asking for his opinion. Here are the points and questions we raised:

Firstly, would dendrochronological tests actually necessitate taking the panel out from its blockboard setting, or could a small section of the blockboard be removed along one edge, thus preventing any danger to the panel?

Secondly, if dendrochronological tests really are impossible to carry out in this case, do you know of any other reliable dating method which could be used successfully without endangering the panel?

What we weren't aware of at the time, was that Professor Hall was Chairman of the National Gallery Honorary Scientific Advisory Committee in 1980, when the painting was being purchased by the Gallery. What ensued should have only been expected: the good professor replied that, unfortunately, he didn't have time to answer our queries properly in detail, but that he had a few comments to share. He answered our questions—most importantly that it *would* be possible to do a dendrochronology test on a 3-mm panel—and expressed that the picture was in his opinion contemporary with Rubens and, indeed, from the artist's own workshop.[6]

OUR REPORT TO THE NATIONAL GALLERY, 1992

On 19 February 1992, Siân, Steve, and I updated our report, and sent it to the recently appointed new Director of the National Gallery, Neil MacGregor. He replied the next day, thanking us and informing us that he had referred the matter to the Head of Flemish Painting, Chief Curator Dr Christopher Brown. We were rather disheartened: we already knew Brown's views on the matter from his publications—he thought it was wonderful! I wanted to copyright our written report to the Gallery, so I chose the easiest way to copyright something: I posted a copy of it registered to myself. I still have the envelope which arrived at my home, unopened.

CORRESPONDENCE WITH DR CHRISTOPHER BROWN

Soon afterwards, Dr Brown wrote us a letter. He acknowledged that our research was, indeed, very thorough. To our surprise, he admitted that the National Gallery could not be "one hundred per cent certain"[7] that theirs was the painting that Rubens painted for Rockox, because the gaps in provenance before and after the Liechtenstein provenance made such an assertion impossible.

WAS THE PRINCE OF LIECHTENSTEIN THE UNDERBIDDER?

In 1980, Margaret Köser put her *Samson and Delilah* (later NG6461) up for auction at Christie's, and on 11 July that year it sold. A third bidder entered the auction, but had to drop out at £1,300,000. From that point on the battle was fought between two bidders. The next day, Geraldine Norman, the saleroom correspondent for *The Times*, wrote: "Christie's hammer fell at £2.3 million; the main competitor was in an anteroom, his bids being relayed to the main saleroom by telephone. The auctioneers would give no indication of his identity yesterday".[8] Sir Geoffrey Agnew, as head of the Bond Street dealers Agnew's, bid for the picture on behalf of the Gallery.

In his letter, Christopher Brown refers to Dr Reinhold Baumstark as a distinguished Rubens authority. But Dr Baumstark is not listed at all among the experts who lent their support to a series of press releases issued by the National Gallery in 1997, and again in 2000, defending the authenticity of the painting. However, in an article in *Apollo* in August 2000 Dr David Jaffé of the National Gallery mentions Dr Baumstark as one of "three Rubens experts who had been contacted by potential purchasers".[9] So, what happened? Was he 'contacted' by the owner of the museum of which he was the Director? Was the late Prince of Liechtenstein really set on 'reacquiring' it for his collection? One would have hoped that a reputable museum prepared to spend such a large sum would have been able to provide some archival documentation in support of the purported provenance—but no such evidence has ever appeared in the bibliography on the painting. Several attempts to contact the Liechtenstein Princely Collections in the late 1980s and early '90s were fruitless.

When I attempted the same again in 2001, the result was different: I received helpful responses from Dr Baumstark's successor, Dr Uwe Wieczorek. He assured me categorically in two letters that, as far as the Collections were aware, the then-Prince of Liechtenstein was *not* the underbidder, nor had he even taken part in the bidding. Since Dr Baumstark, then curator of the collection, is said to have been involved in the attempted re-purchase, we have to believe that the late Prince acted 'off the record'.

We wrote a reply to Dr Brown, the gist of which was that, since he was not sure if the painting was an original, didn't he at least think that a dendrochronology test was in order? In their *Technical Bulletin* of 1983, the National Gallery had explained that they did not want to perform a dendrochronology test in case they jeopardised the safety of the panel, "since the date and provenance of the painting are not in doubt"[10]. However, this did not tally with what Professor Hall had already told us. Christopher Brown never replied to our letter, but he did honour our request four years later, in September 1996.

All that time I continued doing research on this subject, and tried repeatedly to approach journalists in the hope of generating publicity about the matter. One of the people I contacted was Roland Keating of the BBC programme *The Late Show*. In vain.

One evening, several weeks later, I saw Christopher Brown on a special edition of *The Late Show*. Brown was part of a panel that had been invited to discuss the Rembrandt Committee's demotion of a couple of fake Rembrandts in the National Gallery. The National Gallery did not object to this de-attribution, and I couldn't help thinking that this was because the Rembrandts in question had been donated to the museum a century earlier and no reputations were at stake. I remember Brown saying something very glib about how we'd welcome a slimmer, trimmer Rembrandt.

The next day, I wrote a letter to Dr Christopher Brown congratulating him on how good a sport he had been in magnanimously accepting the criticism of the Rembrandt committee. I proposed that he extend his open-mindedness about the National Gallery collection and its fake paintings to Rubens. But, having one unanswered letter pending from him already, I decided not to relive the same experience and never posted this new letter to Brown.

The penny finally dropped when I visited David Lister, arts correspondent for *The Independent*, at his office. After I told him the story, Lister asked me:

"So it's your word against the National Gallery's?"

"I suppose so", I replied.

That was that.

Samson Agonistes

THREATS IN BELSIZE PARK

Just before Christmas 1995, when my Fayum book had just been published, an incident occurred. I was attending a dinner party at the house of a university professor friend in Belsize Park in London. There were just a few couples there, including a very successful architect who knew me. She approached me and asked:

"What are you doing now that your book has come out?"

"Now I'm writing the Rubens book", I replied.

Her expression changed from the suave smile of society small talk to an aggressive, angry glare. Her face said more than her words. She blurted out:

"You must put that away, because they're going to bump you off. It's a mafia—they *will* bump you off, you and your family".

This sort of intimidation—which dates back to 1987—was quite common and is key to understanding my frame of mind. I am not by nature lacking in courage, but repeated incidents like this would unnerve anybody. Since when was having a different opinion about the authorship of a painting a crime?

OVER-RESTORATION & MALPRACTICE

In 1996, I bought a recently published book titled *Art Restoration: The Culture, the Business, and the Scandal* by James Beck[1], Professor of Art History at Columbia University and founding Director of *ArtWatch International* and *ArtWatch Italia*, pressure groups set up to prevent damage to works of art by restorers.

Beck claims that art belongs to all humanity; museums are merely temporary custodians of their treasures and are tasked with looking after them. He discusses the damage caused by over-restoration while paintings are in 'the care' of museums, and includes a scathing attack on the restoration of the ceiling of the Sistine Chapel.

Beck's book featured a chapter written by Michael Daley, the Director of *ArtWatch UK*. In that chapter, Daley criticises the brutal restoration practices of the National Gallery. I couldn't have agreed more with his criticism. It made sense; the pictures in the National Gallery have been so over-cleaned that they have progressively turned from Old Masters into David Hockneys.

The Gallery has been criticised for its approach ever since the first major controversy broke out over its cleaning techniques more than 150 years ago, in 1846. The artist and picture dealer, John Morris Moore, an unrelenting critic of the National Gallery, wrote scathing letters to *The Times* under the pen name Verax[2] about several pictures that had been "subjected to a dreadful ordeal at the cleaner's hands"; one was Titian's *Bacchus and Ariadne*, which had been "scraped raw" in some parts and "repainted in others", while another was Rubens's magnificent *Minerva Protects Pax from Mars ('Peace and War')*, which had been "completely flayed".[3]

A whole group of artists have since been complaining bitterly to the relevant authorities about the brutal over-cleaning of oil paintings with the use of acids. Acids eat away the various layers of old, yellowed varnishes that cover paintings. Unfortunately, they don't stop there. Acids are corrosive, and they continue to eat into the oil paint substructure for an additional period of up to twenty years after their initial application. The touch of the master is lost forever. The baby is thrown out with the bathwater.

I was delighted to learn that there were like-minded people in the artistic community, as well as among the general public, who not only shared the same view on the over-cleaning of paintings and sculptures, but who were actively working to raise awareness of the danger of these practices in museums.

Since Michael Daley lived in England, I thought that it would be a good idea to meet. I asked a mutual friend—a prominent reporter for the *Sunday Times* who thought the story was great—to put us in touch. In the autumn of 1996, I invited Daley and my reporter friend for dinner at a little bistro opposite the British Museum. Siân Hopkinson, one of my two co-authors of the 1992 report on NG6461, came with me.

I didn't bring our report to that first meeting, but we discussed it at length, and Daley asked for more information. I subsequently posted it to him, and he became absolutely convinced that the painting was not by the hand of Rubens. Thus begun a lengthy correspondence between Daley and me. As my research continued, every new discovery was shared with him and added to our ever-expanding list of issues with the painting.

The dialogue with Daley proved extremely productive. We were both passionate about revealing the truth. The channels of communication between Athens and Barnet were on fire: our fax machines were exhausted, our respective spouses were exasperated, and our phone bills reached ever new heights. We had a 'mission impossible' ahead of us: to prove that a painting was not what it was labelled as being, without having the object itself in our hands for examination. If we had had access to NG6461 in a laboratory for a ten-minute technical examination, our task would have been simpler. Without access to the painting, the task was so difficult that anyone in their right mind would have given up long ago.

We made a good team. Daley was meticulous in his surgical dissection of the data, while I was patient and persistent in digging up new evidence. He was delighted with the new information that rolled out of his fax machine on a daily basis. As he told me:

> Usually, when carrying out this kind of research, there is an awful lot of painstaking drudgery before you discover the cherry on top of the cake. But in this case, it's cherry upon cherry upon cherry.

PRINCETON PICTURE LIBRARY

In 1996, after meeting Daley, I spent four months researching Rubens at Princeton University, which has an amazing picture library. I found all the old books on Rubens, dating back to the 1890s, and pored over his entire correspondence in Flemish, Italian, French, and Latin. I also found black-and-white photographs of many *Samson and Delilah* paintings made by various seventeenth-century Flemish artists. I soon realised that every self-respecting painter of that time had had a go at this theme—it was a tremendously popular subject. This strengthened my conviction that Rubens's star students, Jan van den Hoecke and Anthony van Dyck, must surely have produced their own versions of this popular theme, without necessarily copying their master.

While at Princeton, I thought it would be a good idea to meet James Beck, Professor at the time of Art History at Columbia University, whose book on over-restoration had led to my contacting Michael Daley in the first place. Beck had become my hero, as he had already fought a couple of brave battles trying to protect works of art from aggressive over-cleaning by restorers. I rang him and, to my delight, he invited me to New York.

We met in a Starbucks on Broadway, near the university. Daley had already told me about Beck's passionate temperament and total dedication to his chosen course. The first thing Beck said to me, as soon as we shook hands, was "I'm shattered".

He explained over coffee that he was feeling very down because he'd received so many brutal attacks from museum curators and fellow art historians. He felt militant and committed, and still had the energy required for this uphill struggle, criticising institutions where paintings and sculptures were kept, but every now and then he felt beaten.

"Don't worry," he said, "tomorrow I'll be fine. It's so damn difficult!"

I declared total loyalty to his cause. This brought a sudden big smile to his face. The cloudy day lit up. "We will keep up the fight", he said. This time, I felt, with a renewed conviction.

"That *Samson and Delilah* that Michael told me about, I never liked it. It's a terrible scandal. Will you come and talk to my postgrad students in two hours' time?"

"Yes, but my slides are in Princeton" I said.

"You don't need slides. Just tell them the facts".

Beck's students were enthusiastic, and the warmth of his character seemed to have permeated the group. I talked for half an hour and was amazed by how easy it was for me to tell the story. Beck's assistant, an energetic young woman, said that she had been perplexed by NG6461 when she had visited London and the National Gallery just a few days earlier. She said she didn't like it, but had tried to convince herself that she must come round to liking it, since she had read in the National Gallery literature that it was one of Rubens's greatest masterpieces.

"Phew! I am so relieved to hear all this. I thought there was something wrong with me", she told me.

I returned to Princeton feeling enormously heartened by Beck's reaction and the solidarity of this wonderful man.

During this period at Princeton, I also visited Berkeley, California. At Moe's Books, a lovely bookstore in the foothills near the University of California, I found a treasure trove of second-hand books on Rubens. Among them was a recent publication on a colloquium organised by the Tokyo Museum of Western Art. The purpose of the conference had been to decide which of three paintings of *The Flight of Lot and his Family from Sodom* was the original by Rubens.[4] It sounded fascinating, and I grabbed the book off the shelf. Although the results turned out inconclusive, what interested me was the methodology: three versions of the same subject in three different museums, all attributed to Rubens, all brought together in one place for discussion.

Moreover, in 1992, the Getty Kouros, an Archaic Greek statue of disputed authenticity, had been brought to the Museum of Cycladic Art in Athens for a similar expert conference.[5] Again, there was no firm consensus, but the Getty Museum now labels the marble sculpture as follows: "Kouros. Artist/Maker: Unknown. Place: Greece(?) Date: about 530 BC or modern forgery".[6]

In both cases, the museums not only encouraged discussion and published the results but also ensured that the artworks themselves were physically present for scrutiny. This is exactly what should be done with NG6461, but nothing of the sort has ever been proposed—or even considered—by either the National Gallery or the Rubenianum.

Blinded by Science

DALYA ALBERGE'S FIRST ARTICLE IN *THE TIMES*

Back in London, as the connection with *ArtWatch UK* depeened, I started enjoying more credibility than I would have otherwise, and this proved to be critical in finding a platform to publicise the contents of our report.

Michael Daley became an ally. As well as an illustrator and sculptor, Daley is a journalist with good media contacts. He talked to Dalya Alberge, arts correspondent for *The Times*, who proceeded to write three articles about our case over the following two years (1996 and 1997). Initially, we all worked in unison. Although Alberge and I never met, we spoke several times on the phone, and Daley passed on all my written research to her. She was the first journalist who really took the matter seriously.

Alberge published her first article in *The Times* on 19 March 1996. She had called Christopher Brown, then Chief Curator of Dutch and Flemish Painting at the National Gallery, and asked that the Gallery would do a dendrochronology test (a scientific examination that determines when a tree was felled) on NG6461. The following day, her article was published in the Home News section of the newspaper, with a full-colour photograph of the painting and a photograph of Brown, appearing beneath the headline "National Gallery Rubens is Put to The Tree-Ring Test"[1]. The article caused a stir, especially in art circles. The National Gallery eventually responded with a press release.

BRIAN SEWELL

Three weeks after Alberge's article, on 4 July, I received a personal attack by the famously acerbic *Evening Standard* art critic,

Brian Sewell. He was already connected to the case: while working for Christie's, he had organised the sale of the problematic *modello* of the painting in 1966 (as he made sure to mention). Sewell dedicated an entire page to the matter headlined "It's a Real Rubens, Make No Mistake". Incredibly, he proclaimed in his article that he would not accept the tree-ring result even if it proved that the panel was modern. Wrote Sewell:

> I have such profound mistrust of science that if the dendrochronological tests to which the gallery has now consented [...] suggest that the painting was executed at any date other than *c.*1610, I shall take it as proof that the technology is unreliable.[2]

Sewell amusingly says, "There must surely be a proverb warning us against unlikely Greeks expressing improbable opinions". I don't know whether such a proverb exists, but there surely is one about pre-Copernican perceptions of science. And how strange that he should say that when, a few months before, in the same newspaper, he had praised me to the heavens for my Fayum book.[3]

MICHAEL AND DALYA IN THE PRESS: 1997–2006

Articles by Dalya Alberge and Michael Daley continued to appear periodically in the English press. Daley wrote three major articles questioning the authenticity of NG6461 in *Art Review* between 1997 and 2000[4]. The last article provoked a vile personal attack by Brian Sewell, again in the *Evening Standard*[5]. The pattern became apparent: anyone who asked whether this work was by Rubens would a few days later receive a nasty *ad hominem* attack by Sewell in defence of the official National Gallery line.

BROWN'S INVITATION, 1996

After Dalya's first article appeared, and while I was still at Princeton, Dr Christopher Brown wrote to me with news that he had arranged for a dendrochronological analysis. The test would be carried out on NG6461 by Dr Peter Klein, a world-renowned German dendrochronologist, on 25 September 1996. Dr Klein of the University of Hamburg had been employed by the National Gallery before, and they claimed that he was one of the best in his field. I was invited to be present.

I arrived at the Gallery and was met by a large group of people in the Conservation Department, the inside of which I was seeing for the first time. There to greet me was Christopher Brown, as well as members of the Department who I was not familiar with. I was led to a large, high table on which NG6461 lay in state—out of its frame, naked, flat, exposed.

I was surprised to see it look so unimposing—a sliver of veneer-thin wood seemingly stuck on to thick pink modern blockboard, looking 'ironed out' and very unlike what I imagined an original Rubens oak panel would look like.

I already knew from the *Technical Bulletin* of 1983 that the back of the painting had been "planed-down to a thickness of 3 mm and subsequently glued on to a sheet of blockboard"[6]. So it didn't seem surprising that this fine sliver of oak needed to be reinforced by a heavier support: the 3-cm pink blockboard, which protruded about 15 cm around the whole picture seemed an expected and necessary evil in the construction. I was still reeling at the paucity of the object's impact as the painting lay there on the table like a lamb to the slaughter. Dr Klein, in his trim black polo neck jumper, was conscientiously preparing for the operation of extracting a sufficient sample of wood to get results from his test at his laboratory in Hamburg. Holding a scalpel delicately in his right hand, he approached his 'patient'.

Dr Klein pointed out to me that the 3-millimetre-thick wood was attached to the blockboard, as I could clearly see, with a sort of dried putty. He produced a little silver hammer and a small chisel and began hammering away the putty in a certain spot. Minute bangs ensued, *tap tap tap*. "You see, I am breaking the dry putty in order to take the sample from the exposed wood", he explained. Nodding my head in agreement, I assured him that I was following the process.

The only thing I had brought in my handbag was an unashamedly large, round, magnifying glass. I felt a bit like a joke of a detective who was coming to see the painting close up for herself. But while the picture was on the table my fear of being ridiculed stopped me from using it, so I left it in my bag. I later regretted not having used it then and there.

I did, however, pluck up the courage to ask a question:

"Dr Klein, when do you think the painting was planed down and stuck onto this blockboard in its present condition?"

Klein replied: "Around the 1920s".

"But, Dr Klein" I pressed him, "wasn't blockboard invented *after* World War II?"

Klein got into a terrible fluster.

"Yes—'20s, '40s..." he stammered.

There was a long moment of awkwardness, until Christopher Brown stepped forward and said very decisively:

"The painting was planed down before the National Gallery bought it".

For me, it was game, set, and match.

In a very short time, Dr Klein took the meagre sample and told me that we would have the results soon after he had conducted his examination. I did do a quick sketch of the painting off its frame in the few minutes I was left alone with it after the extraction of the sample, then thanked him and said goodbye. I was asked if I wanted to see something else and was taken into another room where a tree trunk was lying on the floor, displaying all the tree rings that dendrochronologists use to determine the year in which a tree was felled. One of the chief conservators stood over me as I somewhat clumsily took out my magnifying glass. Having missed the opportunity earlier to look at the painting through it (and also to take a photograph of the painting out of its frame, which would have proved of enormous help in the following months), I used it to examine the tree rings, something which was hardly necessary as they were quite large and distinct.

I was then led into Dr Brown's office for a short one-on-one discussion. I asked him, "Dr Brown, how do you explain Samson's missing toes?" He simply said, "I do not wish to discuss this matter with you". That was all. There was an awkward silence. I couldn't think what else he might wish to discuss with me, so I just replied, "I see" and rose to leave, thanking him for his time.

I left the National Gallery via the conservation exit, never to cross that threshold again. I had said goodbye to the painting, which I was seeing for the last time laid bare and out of its frame.

DR KLEIN'S RESULTS

Some time later I received the results of the dendrochronology test from Dr Klein. They were two thin lines, the gist of which was that yes, it was possible that the oak tree from which the NG6461 panel was made was felled before 1609. So things were OK according to Klein. I forwarded the results to dendrochronologist

Coralie Mills in Scotland, from whom I commissioned a report. A few weeks later she sent me a very extensive report which outlined the complexity of the situation:[7] Although dendrochronology tests can be valuable, the age of the paint is actually a much more useful test when it comes to determining the date of a painting. Even though old pigments and old oils can be used to make a modern fake, it's much harder to emulate the age of paints.

On the whole, I was very happy to have been given the opportunity to see the painting 'in the flesh', so to speak, off the frame. It revealed the true nature of the object, which I was later able to compare to official reports of how the painting looks today.

10

The Benevolent Banker

After my death, you can use the documents and the photo I gave you.
——Jan Bosselaers

It was Christmas 1996 when Jan Caluwaerts, my brilliant genealogist friend, phoned me from Leuven in Belgium. "We have good news. A gentleman banker phoned me from Antwerp and wants to meet us. He wants to help.".

The banker, Mr Jan Bosselaers, had read a newspaper article in the Flemish press which mentioned that Caluwaerts, a young Flemish man, had helped in the investigation into a painting by Rubens, a 1980 acquisition by the National Gallery in England whose authenticity was being disputed. The Flemish newspaper had picked up Dalya Alberge's first article in *The Times*, written in June 1996. Mr Bosselaers had read about the NG6461 affair and expressed a wish to be of assistance. He knew a lot about the subject because he had been a director of the bank in Antwerp during the reconstruction of the Rockox House (which the bank owned) and had been turned into a museum in 1977 to coincide with the four-hundredth anniversary of Rubens's birth in 1577. Mr Bosselaers, an art lover and connoisseur, had been appointed by the bank to equip the Rockox house with paintings and furniture that would reflect its former glory and its seventeenth-century identity.

Jan informed me that Bosselaers had invited us to the Rockox House for a meeting on 3 January 1997, to give us certain documents that would help us in our quest. How heart-warming that was. Suddenly, the unexpected had happened: amidst all the hostility to our theories, here was someone who was both a lover of art and, apparently, a lover of the truth as well. He was prepared to forsake secrecy and open doors in order to share with us his knowledge of this by-now-infamous painting.

Jan and I turned up at the Rockox house on 3 January. We met Jan Bosselaers and his son Mark, an accomplished painter who taught at the Royal Academy of Fine Arts at Antwerp. Bosselaers led the way up to a conference room under the eaves of what was now the Rockox Museum, with a very long oak table around which we were asked to sit. There were two or three people with us from the museum. Jan, Bosselaers, and I sat at one end of the oblong table, which felt like it spanned the whole room. Just being there in friendly company, up in the attic of Rockox's house, was thrilling.

Bosselaers told me in English that he wanted to help me with my search. He had a stack of papers which he proceeded to place in front of me. "These are for you", he said. I was overwhelmed and thanked him profusely. Now and then he spoke Flemish with Jan, who immediately translated for me: "We have been called here to be given help on our quest", he told me.

Bosselaers's story began to unfold in English. Half the papers he was giving me were from his personal diary and concerned the days preceding the Christie's sale in London in 1980 and, indeed, the day of the sale itself. He and a colleague from the bank had gone to London on 11 July 1980 to bid in the auction for the *Samson and Delilah* (NG6461), which they believed—as did everyone else at the time—to be the original Rockox-owned *Samson and Delilah*. He was outbid at £1.2 million as the price raced upwards, eventually reaching £2.3 million.

He told us that a few months before the sale, the painting had come to Antwerp and had been placed in a vault inside a bank. The owner, Mrs Margaret Köser—the previous owner of NG6461 since 1930—informed Bosselaers that Germany was about to introduce a law prohibiting major works of art from leaving the country. Since she wanted to sell the painting in the near future, she wanted to get it out of the country and would be very grateful if the bank would hold it for safekeeping until such time as the family decided to sell it.

Bosselaers said that the bank had, through him, offered a sum of money to buy the painting from her at that stage, as it would have been a dream scenario for them to place it over the original fireplace in the Rockox Museum, where the original had hung for thirty-one years while Rubens was still alive. But the amount

     NG6461: THE FAKE RUBENS

offered by the bank to Mrs Köser was not accepted, and so the painting ended up in storage at the bank. Bosselaers also mentioned that he had only received the Christie's catalogue a few weeks *after* the London sale—a surprising move on the auction house's part, considering the bank had shown in the past a clear interest in acquiring the work.

Half these papers were photocopies of the correspondence between Mr Bosselaers, Mrs Köser, and Gregory Martin of Christie's in 1980, preceding the Christie's sale. He wanted me to have all this because he knew it would aid my research.

He also said that this was the second time the National Gallery picture had come to Antwerp. The first time was in 1977, when Mrs Köser had lent the painting to the Royal Antwerp Museum of Fine Arts for the retrospective exhibition which took place that year. The organiser of the exhibition was Frans Baudouin, the best-known Rubens scholar at the time, and Head of the Rubenianum.

Bosselaers had inspected NG6461 up-close in 1977, and then again in 1980. Given his familiarity with the painting, I asked him specifically about its back. Bosselaers grabbed a piece of paper and drew a grid of three vertical lines crossed by three horizontal ones. He looked at me.

"A cradle!", I gasped.

"Yes", he said, "it was a cradle".

"Could you describe the panel in more detail?" I went on.

"Yes, at the time that the painting was still on its original panel it ranged in thickness between 2.5 to 4 cm, as one would expect for a Rubens oak panel. It was cradled, reinforced by a wooden lattice, a usual restoration technique used in the nineteenth century. The panel was in very good shape, only warped. The panel was slightly bigger than the painting itself, about 1 to 1.5 cm protruding at each side". As far as he could remember, "an extending piece of light brown wood was glued to the sides of the panel, probably to make it fit the original frame". He described the cradle as having battens which were 4 or 5 cm wide, leaving spaces of about 10 to 15 cm between them. The whole cradled back was painted dark grey, almost black; "it had some labels stuck to it but we didn't pay attention to them".

Bosselaers showed me many photographs of NG6461, taken both times the work had been in Antwerp. One such photo, showing the painting out of its frame, and held up by an employee of the bank, had been taken while it was in safekeeping [36]. In the photo, the painting appeared without the blockboard 'matting' all around it, flush with the edge of the panel.

As soon as I saw it, I exclaimed: "It doesn't look like that now!"

I could see that Mr Bosselaers was surprised and perplexed. "What do you mean?" He said, worriedly.

"I mean that I have seen it off its frame and it has no cradle. It has been stuck onto pink blockboard which protrudes for about 12 cm around the painting, and the painting itself looks like a thin sliver of wood, flat as a pancake. I did a sketch of it *in situ*", I told him, and showed him my sketch **[35]**. And just to assure him, I asked whether this photo he was showing me was truly taken *before* the Christie's sale on 11 July 1980. He answered emphatically in the affirmative.

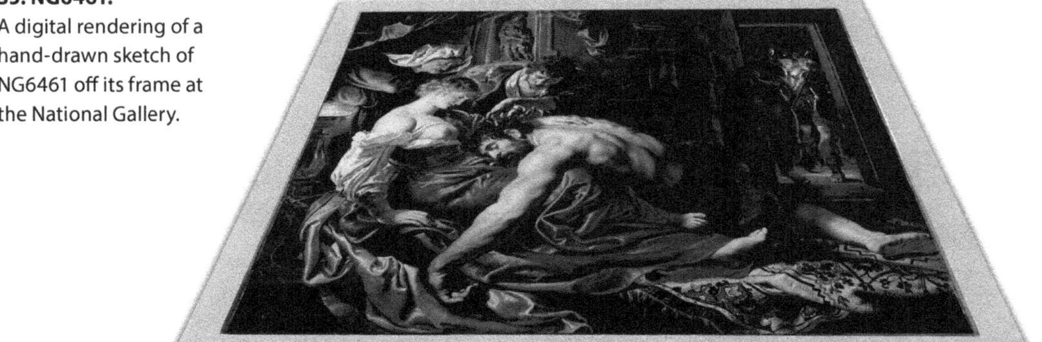

35. NG6461: A digital rendering of a hand-drawn sketch of NG6461 off its frame at the National Gallery.

By this time he looked very worried and began to ask me whether I was certain that it looked different now. I assured him that I had seen it 'in the flesh', and that it was truly a completely different animal now. At this, Bosselaers got up and disappeared for a while, returning twenty minutes later with the President of the bank, who appeared to reside in the same building. He asked me whether I had seen the painting out of its frame and I assured him that I had been invited to the Conservation Department at the National Gallery and had been present, with many witnesses, when the dendrochronology samples had been taken three months earlier.

The President stayed for just five minutes. A lot of Flemish ensued, and Bosselaers told me that the papers and information he had given me, including the photograph, were confidential.

"Confidential until when?" I managed to utter in my great disappointment. "Until the day of my death", he said. I wished him a long life, which happily he was to live. Bosselaers didn't take the confidential material away from me; he trusted that I would respect his wishes. Apart from not wanting to betray his trust, I also knew that going against his wishes would be litigious.

While we were still in Antwerp, Bosselaers invited Jan and me to his home. His wife was a very kind lady. After dinner, she looked me in the eyes and told me that she was horrified by what she had heard about the painting. "How shocking that it now looks different from the photograph." I agreed with her.

I left Antwerp feeling that fate had once again decided that my odyssey would not be coming to an end anytime soon.

Years later, in 2008, I saw Mr Bosselaers again in the Rockox House, this time on the occasion of the NG6461 having been sent by the National Gallery to hang over the fireplace for an exhibition advertised all over Antwerp as a momentous event.[1] His son Mark was there too, and we posed together for a photograph under the fake painting which, incidentally, was clearly way too small for the wall.

The inventory made on the death of Rockox and the announcement of the public auction held the following year, in 1641, made no mention of the actual size of the painting. But we can very accurately calculate the dimentions of the original painting by comparing it to the fireplace's size in the Franken painting. However, the 2008 exhibition display had been set up in a perplexing way: shelves had been purposely built that bisected the great salon, jutting bizarrely out into the middle of the room. The result was that you could not see NG6461 distinctly on its own above the fireplace in the normally empty rectangle of the salon, so familiar from the Frans Francken *Kunstkammer* painting.

After posing for the photograph, I went for a coffee with Bosselaers and some other people. I was expecting to be thanked for having respected his confidentiality request for so many (more than ten) years. For me, impatient as I am, it had seemed like a century. This expression of gratitude never came, so I decided that perhaps if I gave Bosselaers a copy of my manuscript on the Rubens affair and my involvement in it, he might realise how important it was to me, and how crippling this prohibition had been. I asked him to have a look at it and let me know his thoughts, but I never heard back.

Seven years later, in July 2015, I was surprised to see on the internet that Jan Bosselaers, aged ninety-seven, had appeared on Belgian public television saying that he wanted to make public the secret about a painting. It flashed through my mind that he had decided to publicise the NG6461 scandal, which he knew so much about. This thought was quickly dispelled, however, when I read on that Bosselaers was referring to a different story altogether: he wanted to let the people of Belgium, and the whole world, know that the famous van Eyck Ghent Altarpiece panel (which had been stolen in the 1930s and never seen since) had been offered to his bank for purchase by the heirs of the thieves! The bank had made an offer which the sellers didn't accept.

A couple of years later, in 2017, I read Mr Bosselaers's obituary on the internet. The confidentiality restrictions on the documents he had given me were lifted. I was finally free to publish all the documents, including the all-revealing photograph **[36]**.

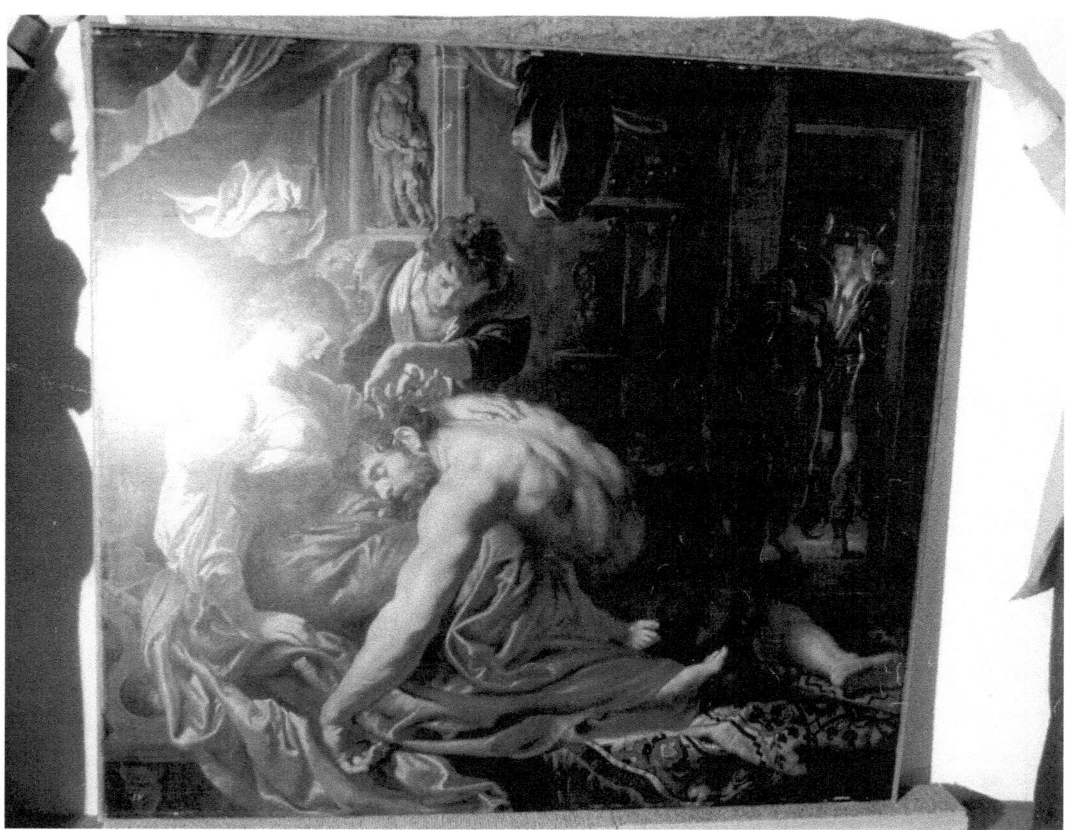

36. NG6461:
The contested Rubens photographed in 1980 before the Christie's sale, and while in the hands of the late Jan Bosselaers.

    NG6461: THE FAKE RUBENS

11

Reversal of Fortune

The truth will come out in the end—it always does!
—— Isaiah Berlin

Greeks have an entertaining proverb which goes: "in my misfortune I had a stroke of luck". I always felt that this applied to me in my long quest for the truth about the painting. On so many occasions over the years, wonderful discoveries have been followed by great disappointments. The way is never smoothly paved. I say this because, when I first set out on this quest to discover the truth about NG6461, I never imagined, or dreamt, or dared to dream, that I would be propped up along the way by one of last century's greatest minds. But I was. The events are as follows.

In 1997, after several publications on the subject of NG6461 in the British press, I was invited to dinner with Sir Isaiah Berlin and his wife, on the occasion of his being awarded an honorary doctorate by the University of Athens. It was my friend Nedis Dimitrakos and his wife, the wonderful art historian Marilena Cassimatis, who invited me to the Athinaiki Leschi (Athens Club) after the ceremony. There were three couples: Sir Isaiah and Lady Berlin, Nedis and Marilena, and my partner and me.

I found myself sitting next to this unique man, then already in his eighties. I knew that he had been one of the Trustees of the National Gallery in 1980 when NG6461 was purchased. I also knew the National Gallery's procedures on purchasing artworks, namely that, before the Gallery goes ahead with a purchase, the Trustees must be shown the work in question, which has to be physically brought to them to inspect and approve. Marilena discussed many art history subjects with Sir Isaiah in German.

The conversation sounded really interesting, but the language barrier meant I couldn't follow it. Sir Isaiah looked animated and seemed to be enjoying the evening very much. I wanted to ask him about NG6461, but I was mindful to steer clear of controversy at a friendly dinner table. However, the temptation was eventually too great to resist. Five minutes before the end of the meal, and when I was sure that only Marilena and I had his attention, I leaned towards him, and in a rather low voice for a Greek, I said: "Sir Isaiah, I am the unpleasant person who is doubting the authenticity of the National Gallery Rubens *Samson and Delilah* painting". I purposely made my question long-winded enough to allow him time to think about how to react to this sudden bolt out of the blue. He listened attentively, and I took advantage of his silence to continue: "I believe that you may have been a Trustee in 1980 when the Gallery acquired the painting at Christie's". He immediately retorted: "I don't remember the Gallery buying a Rubens while I was a Trustee there". I understood his signalling that we had to close the subject, and thanked him.

Five minutes later, we all got up to leave. Some of the party headed to the cloakroom to collect their coats, passing in front of an eerie piano which was playing away without a pianist. Sir Isaiah walked on between Marilena and me. Suddenly, in an animated voice, he turned and said to me, "I'll help you with the Rubens! I'll tell you who to write to. You will write to the President of Corpus Christi College, Oxford, Keith Thomas. You will write to him *from me* and you will tell him *from me* that the truth will come out in the end—it always does!"

The next morning, Marilena phoned me to say that, on their way to Berlin's hotel, he confided to her: "Your friend is right about the Rubens. People like that usually are". What a lightning bolt this was! Ten years after embarking on this quest, I finally felt vindicated.

But it was not to be. A few weeks later, as I was still fumbling with correcting the language in the letter I was writing to Sir Keith Thomas, I learnt the sad news that Sir Isaiah Berlin had passed away. My heart sank. Accompanying the sadness of his passing was an overwhelming sense of disappointment that an important ally in this dark period of fighting for the truth was now gone.

It was too late! My letter from him could no longer be sent. It was certainly not easy to recover from this blow. After having finally had my quest of so many years unequivocally endorsed by an insider of such enormous repute, I felt utterly deflated by his sudden loss.

Regardless, the personal experience with Sir Isaiah had boosted my morale. Someone who thought and wrote so extensively about the notions of freedom, truth, and integrity had assured me that I was right! Thinking back on it, I thought how characteristic of his mind were the words he had said to me: "The truth will come out in the end—it always does!"

12

The Dictatorship of Experts

Back in 1997 I had gone back to London to tell Michael Daley and Dalya Alberge what that had happened in Antwerp. I rang Mark Bosselaers and asked him if he would talk to Alberge, who wanted to write an article about the latest evidence we had gathered. Mark said that he couldn't. He also added that his father did not want to speak to the press or make any statements about the matter.

I started getting legal advice to see whether the documents that Bosselaers had given me could be publicised without legal ramifications. My solicitors advised me that in Belgium publishing confidential documents is a criminal offence. In truth, I was more concerned about not upsetting the banker and his family, and about keeping my word to him.

"YOUR INFORMANT IS WRONG"

Regardless, thanks to Bosselaers's information and the picture he had shown me, I now knew for sure that the painting had been cut down after 1980, even if I was unable to share this knowledge publicly for fear of breaching my confidentiality promise. A familiar feeling of menace was revived, so I decided to let the matter rest for a while.

Both Daley and Alberge shared the sentiment that these Belgian facts had to be kept quiet. Daley decided to open a line of correspondence with Neil MacGregor, Director of the National Gallery. He asked MacGregor whether the painting was now flush to the edge. MacGregor replied that indeed it was, referring to whoever had supplied Daley with intelligence to the contrary as an informant. Daley, who had never seen the painting off the frame with his own eyes, trusted my judgement and, of course, my description. I, on the other hand, had been demoted from a well-meaning researcher and a guest at the public institution's Conservation Department a few weeks earlier to an *informant*.

Daley then followed up with MacGregor, asking to see photographs of the back of the blockboard on which the picture was mounted. The photographs were indeed sent, together with a request that they be returned.

DATING THE BLOCKBOARD

Daley contacted an expert on materials, the Director of the National Panel Products Division in the UK, Charles Norman, a specialist on blockboards, sending him the high-resolution photographs that the National Gallery had provided. Norman told Daley that the blockboard on the back of the painting must be relatively new—perhaps as recent as the 1970s. With this report in hand, Dalya Alberge published a new article quoting him.[1]

When the Gallery saw Alberge's article, they called a meeting with Norman. What was discussed in this meeting has remained undisclosed to third parties. What we do know is that, following that meeting, the National Gallery commissioned its own report on the age of the blockboard from another certification company, called BM TRADA. When this arrived, Daley was notified that it had reached a different conclusion regarding the board's date. It claimed the blockboard was from the 1940s.

DALYA ALBERGE ACCUSES THE NATIONAL GALLERY

Some time later, Alberge published a fourth article, in which she outright accused the National Gallery of cutting the painting. This was the first direct attack against the age-old institution. I had no part in the writing of this article, since Alberge didn't have the banker's permission to make this information public, and I obviously didn't want to compromise my position. If the National Gallery had decided to take this to court, it would become a *cause célèbre* and they would have to have the painting properly inspected by independent experts.

Then, at the beginning of 1997, Michael Daley made a more specific accusation: he began to write about the back of the picture, the oak panel that had supposedly been planed down to three millimetres, and to speculate with convincing precision about who had reduced the panel and when they had done it. Things got worse. The National Gallery condescended to write the first press release answering their critics only after Daley's attack in *The Times*, in an article written by Dalya Alberge.[2]

KASIA PISAREK, SIMON SCHAMA

A big shock came one Sunday morning when Daley phoned me at my home in Athens to tell me that the *Sunday Times* had a huge article in the colour supplement, as well as an annex to the main article on page 8 of the Home News section.[3] The author, Waldemar Januszczak, presented the research of a Polish scholar named Kasia Pisarek, who was unknown to me at the time but later became a dear friend and colleague. She had come to the same conclusions regarding the inauthenticity of NG6461 as us. Her research extended to more paintings in the collection of August Neuerburg, and she went on to write her Ph.D. thesis at the University of Warsaw on that very subject a few years later.[4] One of the chapters is on the major problems with NG6461.

In the ensuing weeks we didn't try to publish anything, but I continued sharing my research with *ArtWatch* and occasionally exchanging faxes and friendly chats with Michael Daley. It was during this time that I found out that I couldn't lay the ghost to rest. By then I had a room in the centre of Athens full of research—it had long since burst out of my suitcase—which had cost me thirteen years of painstaking reading, note-taking, and financial outlay. There was a mass of correspondence, as well as articles written in the press about the Rubens affair, and photographs and books which substantiated my theory.

I would have left it at that, but in 1999 a book by Simon Schama called *Rembrandt's Eyes* hit the bookshops.[5] Dr Schama did me the great honour of mentioning me in one of the footnotes of his hefty volume, in which I was heralded as the main objector to the authenticity of NG6461. He described me as an Egyptologist. And yet in my book on the Fayum portraits from Egypt, I had explained that I was not an Egyptologist at all, but a painter who approached this fascinating subject from the point of view of an artist. Schama described my reasons for thinking that the painting in question was not authentic as coming down to an inadequate execution and an uncharacteristic set of brushstrokes. Without bothering to seek my views on the matter, he seemed content to base his remarks on hearsay.

Michael Daley dedicated issue 11 of the *ArtWatch Newsletter* in Autumn 2000 to the controversy. He asked a friend (a former member of Christie's staff) to inquire about the picture's condition when it was held by the auction house, and that friend found out that Brian Sewell (who had discovered the supposed *modello*) remembered it there in 1980: the original back survived, and was cross-battened; it was painted in a matte, blackish colour; and the 'cradle' was not a proper cradle because its crossed bars could not slide one against the other when the panel expanded or contracted with changes in humidity. His account was consistent with the catalogue, where the picture was described as a 'panel'.

In April 1997, Daley had informed Neil MacGregor of this testimony, and asked whether the Gallery had any record of the condition and appearance of the back *before* its planing.[6] MacGregor had replied two days later that Daley's sources were mistaken and that the structure of the painting had not been altered since its sale at Christie's in 1980.[7] But Daley insisted: did the Gallery have "any record—photographic or written" of the painting's back before it was planed down? The answer soon came back and it was flatly in the negative. The planing, it was alleged, was done in the twentieth century, perhaps in the 1920s, in Paris. But we know that in fact it was certainly done after 1930, since we now have Burchard's authenticity report of that year, which assures us that the back of the panel was still in its original state at that time.

In the 1980 National Gallery Annual Review, Michael Levey, then Director, thanked Christie's for their co-operation in allowing the Trustees to see this painting in the Gallery before the sale and by doing so assess the work's powerful impact and its major contribution to the painter's representation. In a letter to Michael Daley on 27 May 1997, MacGregor now confirmed that the painting had been examined "in the flesh" before the sale, but not that the Trustees had inspected it, and it was further confirmed that Christopher Brown and Martin Wyld had done the examination and that there was widespread recollection (including by Christie's staff) that the panel was set into blockboard.

Why, Michael Daley wondered, was MacGregor citing the *recollections* of Dr Brown and Mr Wyld? Had they not written a report? Had they alone, and not the Trustees, inspected the painting? And *ArtWatch*'s source could not recall having been shown the picture.

Early in 2000, Neil MacGregor, reversing an eight-year-long policy, allowed Michael Daley to examine the National Gallery's conservation and historical dossiers on NG6461. Three years prior, in his 27 May 1997 letter, he had enclosed photographs of the back of NG6461 "as it is now".

Two of the photographs were close-ups, supposedly showing 'labels' fixed to the blockboard backing. One—which certainly is a label—was said to have been attached in 1977 at the time of the great Antwerp Rubens exhibition. It shows signs of having been attacked with a scraper. The other—which appears not to be a label, but part of a page of typescript—was described as being "from the Neuerburg Collection" and to have been applied somewhat earlier.[8] Both 'labels' appeared not to be pasted on the blockboard but instead to be held against it by transparent film fixed with clear masking tape. Both cast shadows on the backing—not something common for labels.

The photographs were said to show the "dirty grey painting, on which is stencilled Christie's number"[9]. A former member of Christie's staff to whom the photographs were shown was bemused, since he had never encountered such a method of labelling. Moreover, he said, a picture with a back in such condition, at that date, would not have been described by Christie's as a 'panel' but as a 'reduced (or 'thinned') panel laid on blockboard'. Brian Sewell was similarly bemused. Not only had the back of the picture not been in its present condition in 1980, but the Christie's number had been stencilled on to a white patch painted on to the picture's then-black back.

Surely a record of Burchard's examination of the picture in 1930 must exist, Michael Daley thought, and surely enough it did: Daley found a copy of it in the Gallery's dossier. In that document, Burchard testified that the picture was "in a remarkably good state of preservation"—and that "even the back of the panel is in its original condition"!

DAVID JAFFÉ'S REPLY

The August 2000 *Apollo* included a reply to the *ArtWatch Newsletter* examination: a long article by David Jaffé of the National Gallery titled "Rubens Back And Front"[10], in which Jaffé attempted to prove that the remounting on blockboard had been done during the Neuerburg period—which, after all, had always seemed the most likely explanation. He argued that this technique, known as 'marouflaging', was common practice in Germany between the wars and that a high percentage (though not all) of the Neuerburg pictures were given this treatment. Other Neuerburg pictures sold through Christie's (but not NG6461) were described as "set in marouflage panels". Daley, in the *Art-Watch Newsletter* of Autumn 2000, pointed out, quite correctly, that none of this amounted to proof that the marouflaging had been done for Neuerburg.

"THE BACK IS WHERE IT'S AT"

Daley started collecting material for another article about the back of the painting: "The Back Is Where It's At"[11]. The *Independent on Sunday* ran a preview of this article, together with a colour photo, at the end of May. This time, all hell broke loose. Daley quoted Brian Sewell as a witness who had seen the painting before the sale at Christie's and had reported that it was cradled, just as the banker in Antwerp had told me. Brian Sewell had not been revealed as a witness in the *Sunday Times* article. A storm of letters in the press ensued between Michael Daley, Brian Sewell, and Neil MacGregor. Even I wrote a couple whenever I couldn't keep my mouth shut. Sewell denied everything he had told Daley, and wrote a libelous text in the *Evening Standard*—a personal attack against Michael Daley titled "To a Dabbler in the Dark"[12]. Like his attack on me a few years before, Sewell was both menacing and deceitful, in that he went back on his word to Daley: although he had given him permission to quote him, he denied all when he was quoted and his writing about NG6461 itself was in terribly bad taste.

Daley was, understandably, very upset. To be decried in this way was a real shock. He decided not to sue Brian Sewell and instead wrote a letter to the newspaper in his own defence—as did I. Needless to say, neither of our letters was published by the *Evening Standard*. Daley had been dealt a terrible blow; he lost his column in *Art Review*, which happened to change editor at exactly the same time. However, The *Independent on Sunday* printed both Daley's and my letter. In mine, I attacked Baudouin for the first time: in the 1977 catalogue of the Rockox House, Baudouin gives an inaccurate and misleading provenance. There is no evidence to show that the original painting by Rubens was not lost in 1641.

THE PAINTING'S BACK IN 1980

The final question is: what did the back look like in 1980 when the Gallery bought the picture? Here the evidence is strangely conflicting. In the end, I consider my own experience to be the most valid contradiction to what the National Gallery is professing about the panel and its condition. It is my word against theirs.

THE FRAME

Related to this is the mystery of the frame. In their catalogue, Christie's had described the frame as being "similar to" and perhaps "identical with" the one recorded in Frans Francken's depiction of Rockox's great salon.[13] The National Gallery, admirably, goes to great lengths to obtain appropriate period frames for its paintings. In his Pocket Guide, *Frames*, Dr Nicholas Penny of the National Gallery speaks of the "perfect marriage" that is sometimes achieved between a picture and its frame. He laments the fact that many a frame, even after centuries of loyal but discreet service, has been "carelessly discarded"[14]. Yet the frame on NG6461 when it emerged from conservation was new. No explanation has been given for the discarding of the old frame in which the painting was acquired. Was it retained by the Gallery? Did it cease to fit the picture? In the indistinct world of National Gallery pronouncements, sadly, anything is possible.

The Massacre of the Innocents

On 10 July 2002, a Rubens painting was auctioned by Sotheby's. This was going to be a ghostly rerun of the *Samson and Delilah* auction at Christie's twenty-two years earlier, almost to the day. This time the painting was *The Massacre of the Innocents*, a gory subject at the best of times. As Maev Kennedy, *The Guardian* arts correspondent, commented, "Rubens's treatment was so bloody, with mothers and soldiers knee-deep in dead babies, that the painting stayed out of gaze for centuries"[1].

In the Sotheby's sale catalogue, twenty-three pages are dedicated to Lot 6, *The Massacre of the Innocents*. Interestingly, they include a colour reproduction of NG6461; even more interestingly, the *Massacre* was brought to the National Gallery before the auction so that the two paintings could be studied side by side. As Kennedy wrote, "they are so closely related in style and technique that they must stand or fall by the same attribution". What was going on?

The documentation provided by the saleroom this time was spectacularly more detailed than that provided by Christie's twenty-two years earlier, and it included reproductions of the back, and of the Liechtenstein seals. Unlike the Christie's catalogue, it was widely distributed to interested parties well in advance of the auction. Technical analyses and condition reports were also made available in a separate, very comprehensive and elaborately produced and illustrated, hardback book.

The Sotheby's catalogue explains: "The *Samson and Delilah*, sold by the Liechtensteins in circa 1880, was recognised as by Rubens in the 1920s, but the present *Massacre of the Innocents* was assumed to be by Jan van den Hoecke until a few weeks ago".

The misattribution of both paintings, we are told, seems "to depend largely on the whim of [the Liechtenstein catalogue's] painter-compiler, Vincenzio Fanti". "The mis-identification seems strange to us today", the catalogue continues, "but Rubens's early style was not so well understood until recently, and Jan van den Hoecke (1611–1651), though little known now, was for a while the foremost exponent of Rubens's style in Vienna, where he was much in demand". However, his "dry classicizing style and the attenuated figures [...] are far removed from the *Massacre of the Innocents*, or the London *Samson and Delilah*, the picture first burdened with an attribution to van den Hoecke".[2]

This confident-sounding passage contains a number of curious statements. First, the date when the Liechtenstein *Samson and Delilah* (NG6461) was sold ("in circa 1880"): the cataloguer must have been aware that 1880 (the date confidently given by Christie's) had been superseded by a more accurate dating provided by the collection's director, namely 1881. Then there is the leap of faith: the Liechtenstein picture "was recognised as by Rubens in the 1920s": as we have seen, there is absolutely no evidence that connects the unknown seller in Paris in 1929 with the Liechtenstein Collections. Further, we are told that the misattribution of both works seems "to depend largely on the whim of the painter-compiler, Vincenzio Fanti". The phrase "painter-compiler" is clearly intended to discredit Fanti. But it should be remembered that, before the rise in the nineteenth century of art history as a discipline, one looked for such information to painters, connoisseurs, and dealers with a good eye. And, in any case, Fanti's "whim" did not determine the attribution, since the *Samson and Delilah* had entered the collection in 1674 as a van den Hoecke! And, as with the *Massacre*, are we to unquestioningly accept that the compilers of the 1780 and 1873 Liechtenstein catalogues mindlessly adopted Fanti's faulty attribution, the latter a whole century later?

Finally, there is the reassuring reference to "Rubens's early style", "not so well understood until recently" and therefore open to misidentification. But, can it really account for the radical difference in appearance between the two works: NG6461, angular and flat; and the *Massacre*, swirling and dynamic?

Like NG6461, *The Massacre of the Innocents* was another painting from the Liechtenstein Collection (in this case, without a doubt) that had previously been attributed to Jan van den Hoecke and was suddenly promoted to a Rubens. It is interesting to note the lessons that had apparently been learnt since the NG6461 sale. The *Massacre* was accompanied by full documentation on the painting's provenance and condition, and by detailed photographs, answering many of the questions that have been asked in vain about NG6461.

When I wrote to Dr Uwe Wieczorek back in 2001, I asked him whether there was ever a Rubens *Samson and Delilah* in the Liechtenstein Collections before 1880. Dr Wieczorek replied that no *Samson and Delilah* by Rubens had ever been in the Collection.

SOTHEBY'S AUCTION

I wanted to feel first-hand the atmosphere of the sale which I had missed at Christie's in 1980, when NG6461 had been sold for £2.5 million. Having dedicated the previous fifteen years to researching that picture, I was eager to experience the intoxicating atmosphere of a high-stakes sale. The last time I had been present at such an over-hyped auction was when van Gogh's *Sunflowers* had been sold at Christie's in 1987. Talk about eroticising money!

I managed to reserve seats for myself and Siân Hopkinson at the Sotheby's evening sale of *The Massacre of the Innocents*. The room was packed with well-dressed people, and the auctioneer was the elegant and theatrical Henry Wyndham. The estimated value was £4–6 million, and the auctioneer began at £3 million. The figure gradually rose to £10 million; then there was a clear run, rising million by million in seconds.

"Thirty-seven, thirty-eight, thirty-nine, forty, forty-one, forty-two, forty-three, forty-four…" Then a lull. You couldn't hear anyone breathing. One of the two final bidders braved it:

"Forty-four and a half million pounds". Everyone gasped. It looked as though the bidder in the front row had prevailed, when the smart gentleman standing to my left surprised everyone by securing the deal for an anonymous buyer.

"At forty-five million, at forty-five million, sold at forty-five million pounds!" The hammer went down. There was a rush of spontaneous applause, and shouts of "Bravo, bravo!" The mystery buyer was a star. What evil genius could spoil it all by coming along and saying that the painting wasn't by Rubens after all?

So *The Massacre of the Innocents* sold for £45 million, or £49,950,000 with the buyer's premium. It was the most expensive Old Master sold at auction at the time—in 1980, NG6461 had been the second most expensive of its time. It soon emerged that the buyer was the Canadian billionaire media magnate and art collector Lord Kenneth Thomson. He immediately loaned the *Massacre* to the National Gallery for three years, where it was displayed in the same room as NG6461 before being moved to the Thomson Collection at the Art Gallery of Ontario, of which it is now the centrepiece. What an expensive show of solidarity.

Rubens in Abyssinia Square

Early one morning in 2003, while I lay awake worrying about how an unsavoury exchange I had had with a British newspaper would play out, I decided to take a walk in rainy Athens. I headed from my home near Syntagma Square down the hill towards Monastiraki. I walked into Abyssinia Square, the location of the Sunday flea market.

The first thing I saw, leaning against a wall and with its base on a blanket covered with second-hand bric-a-brac, was a huge, round, copper repoussé relief of Peter Paul Rubens in his exquisite hat, exactly as he appears in one of his self-portraits. I did a double take and read the words running around the portrait: "Petrus Paulus Rubens", as he signed himself.

"Who is this portrait of?" I asked the vendor.

"I don't know", he said, "my sister who lives in Brussels sent it to me".

I asked him the price. "60 euros".

I didn't enter the proverbial practice of haggling. I felt that this was a sign from Rubens himself not to give up. What a find at what a moment! I hastily unbuckled the cheap Swatch off my wrist and gave it to the vendor, saying:

"I'll be back at two o'clock to get this, please don't sell it to anyone else. I don't have the money on me right now but I'll go get it".

As agreed, I returned later with the money, and as I handed the notes to the seller I suddenly felt a pain in my chest that I mistook for a heart attack. It had begun to rain, my hand was outstretched with the money, and my chest was hurting. I said to the vendor:

"Please get me some water, and I need something to sit on". As if by some miracle, the man instantly handed me a small bottle of water and I felt a chair being placed under me to sit on. It was astonishing that help came so quickly.

I gulped down the entire contents of the bottle, and very soon I felt that the storm had passed. The smiling face of the merchant giving me back my Swatch was comforting. I took the metal roundel under my arm and, assuring him that I was OK, began to walk up the slight hill towards home. I now had with me Peter Paul Rubens, who had just given me the message: "Don't abandon me. I'm here. Hang in there!"

These occurrences might seem like a silly detour, but for a single person mounting an attack of the scale of the *Samson and Delilah* affair these Rubens-related coincidences that have occurred over the years have been a true source of inspiration and encouragement and have helped me to keep going with my quest. A journalist once asked me, "Are you obsessed with the Rubens affair?". "No", I replied, "Just persistent".

Canvassing Opinion

"IT'S LINEN!"

In the late 1980s, I purchased a very expensive professional Zeiss monocular to scrutinise the painting in the National Gallery, since photography was not allowed at the time. This tool enabled me to see a level of detail on the painting that would otherwise have required a telephoto lens.

Subsequently, in 1989, I heard of a very accomplished wood-polisher (whose request for anonymity I shall respect) who had just arrived in London from Spain. I have always thought that knowledge of materials comes best from hands-on experience, so I asked her to visit the Gallery and examine the painting with me. She agreed to join me, not knowing anything about the controversy that was already surrounding NG6461.

When we stood in front of the painting, I gave her the monocular and asked her to tell me whether she thought it was painted on oak or some other type of wood. After spending more than an hour carefully examining every inch of the painting, both through the monocular and with the naked eye, she finally said, "I'm ready". We went up to the painting together and stood just a metre away, as close as we were allowed. Keeping her voice down, she turned and said to me: "It's not wood. It's fabric. And I will show you why".

She took me aside to sit on the bench and drew up a quick sketch of the panel as seen from the side. The National Gallery claims that the wooden panel is comprised of five or six planks joined together (both 'five' and 'six' planks are mentioned in the *Technical Bulletin*, and 'six' in previous published descriptions). There should in that case be a pitch-black, hairline gap between the panels, which is typical of paintings executed on the satin-smooth surface of an oak panel—as one can observe in so many works by Rubens in the same room and particularly in his landscapes. On this one, however, there was absolutely no trace of any such gap(s). As she demonstrated in her sketch—and as I saw myself once I knew what to look for—when the surface of the painting is seen in section, the canvas forms a curved dip between each pair of planks, as cloth does when you cover something.

I was delighted that, without any external influence, her analysis had perfectly explained the interwoven pattern I had observed on the painting's surface. I instinctively went over to look again at the label next to the painting, just to make sure I hadn't missed anything. There it was in black on white: "oil on *oak* panel" (my emphasis). Could it be that the National Gallery was so shockingly mistaken?

In hindsight, I kick myself for not having realised there and then, at that early stage, that this observation was the key to answering the entire authenticity question. Had I taken this find of my expert witness to its logical conclusion, it would have settled the matter for good. But since photography was not allowed, and since high-resolution cameras were not widely available at the time, I thought, "how do we make others see this too?"

At the time, I couldn't have imagined that, by the year 2020, technology would have moved fast enough to make it possible to take high-resolution photos of the surface of the painting that would unequivocally reveal the canvas texture. Nor could I have foreseen that, during the COVID-19 lockdown, I would still be trying to demonstrate the truth about the materials and asking restorers to confirm it.

HIGH-RESOLUTION PHOTOGRAPHS

In 2019, I gave a draft of my book to someone whose profession is solving real-life puzzles. He was intrigued by the account of my trials and tribulations over what were at the time thirty-two years of research on NG6461. Interestingly, that person is descended from a long line of Irish clothmakers, so the question of the material attracted his attention. His first remark on reading my text was: "You have the answer right there in the book. You say it's on linen! If it is linen and you prove it, you will have achieved your goal. You will have shown that this could *not* be the original Rubens painted for Nicolaas Rockox in 1609, which was, according to every source, including the original inventory made at Rockox's death, an 'oil painting on oak panel'".

Buoyed by my friend's statement, I decided to investigate further. In 2020, just before the outbreak of the coronavirus, I was in London. I went to Jessops on Oxford Street to buy a professional high-resolution camera. That proved to be out of my budget, but I did find a good enough 20-megapixel camera with a high-resolution lens. I bought it and went straight to the National Gallery, where photography was by that time allowed. I took as many photos of the surface of the painting as I could fit in the memory card. Luckily, the painting was at the time lit by a spotlight placed directly above it. The beam of light 'shaved' across the surface and picked up all the details of the relief, with what is known to restorers as 'raking light' [37, 38]. The high-resolution photographs revealed what in the lower right-hand corner—where the painting meets the frame—appeared to be a linen edge.

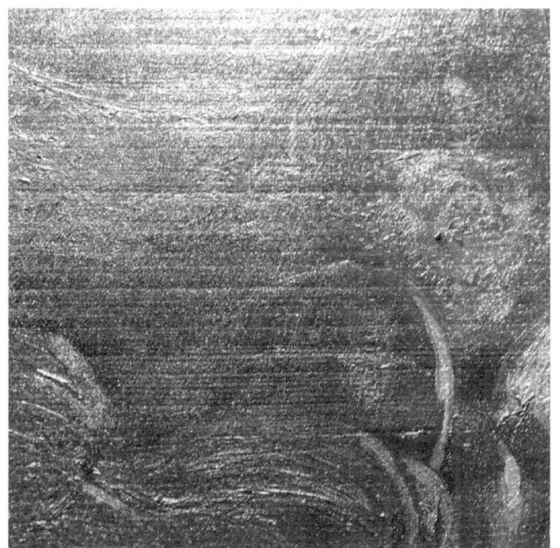
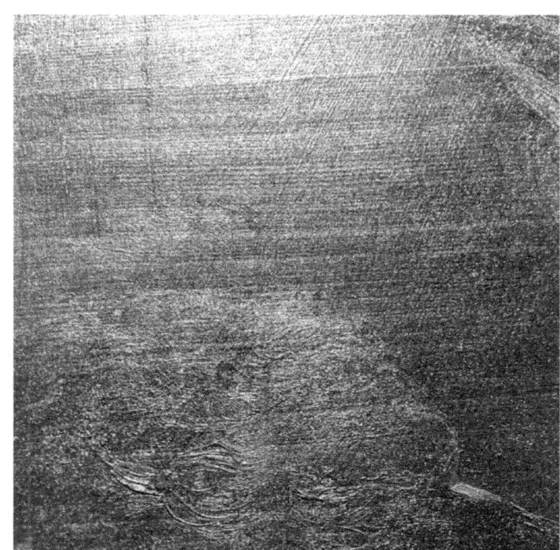

37, 38. NG6461 (details): Photographs taken of the painting by the author which reveal the surface's woven texture.

GEORGIOS BOUDALIS

I thought to approach professional conservators and restorers for their opinion on the painting's surface. Nine out of ten did not want to get involved, for fearing of speaking out against the so-called 'establishment'. I was all too familiar with this response, because so many people I had approached over the years prior had similarly opted out. Finally, I asked a good friend and brilliant archaeologist, Angeliki Kottaridi, who was part of Manolis Andronikos's legendary excavation of the royal tomb of Philip II

     CANVASSING OPINION

of Macedon, the father of Alexander the Great, in Vergina. She was at the time Director of the local Ephorate of Antiquities and suggested I get in touch with the renowned conservator Georgios Boudalis.

I knew Georgios as a conservator of world-class stature. He was the obvious person to ask, but I hadn't thought of contacting him before. Georgios studied painting conservation in Florence and Athens, and also holds a doctorate from the University of the Arts London, making him distinctly qualified to comment on paintings and their structure. He was at the time the Head of Book Conservation at the Museum of Byzantine Culture of Thessaloniki, and a team leader of the St Catherine's Library Conservation Project at the Monastery of St Catherine in Sinai. When I reached out to him he mentioned that he was already familiar with the painting and had seen it before, *in situ*, at the National Gallery. He was keen to examine my high-resolution photographs of the painting's surface, in order to determine whether it was canvas or wood.

As soon as he'd examined my files, Georgios phoned me and said, "I think I agree with you. The texture of the surface is obviously oil painted on canvas, but I will let you know more conclusively after closer examination. Would it be alright if I sent this to my Italian restorer contacts, whose opinion I trust, without telling them which painting it's of?"

"Of course", I said. The four colleagues that he asked came back with a mixture of positive and sceptical responses. Some of them did say they agreed with us, that this was oil on canvas, but some couldn't—or wouldn't—say for sure.

Georgios told me,

I'll send you specific pictures with details but I want to state that what makes it certain that this has been painted on canvas is the way the oil paint follows the undulations of the threads in the cloth. It grips the canvas by adhering to the threads and to the gaps between the threads. This is what definitively proves that this has been painted on canvas.[1]

If it had been painted on a prepared wooden panel, especially an oak panel, the paint would not grip but would sit on the surface in a totally different way.

     NG6461: THE FAKE RUBENS

STÉPHANE TREILHOU

Following this exciting affirmation, I contacted a professor of art at the American University in Paris, Stéphane Treilhou, who in 2018, while standing in front of NG6461, had texted me: "It's linen!" Stéphane teaches a course on the materials and techniques of Renaissance artists, so he is well qualified to speak on the matter. He also makes clavichords, so he knows a lot about wood. In 2020, I sent him my high-resolution images of the painting's surface. This was his response:

> From the photographs I have been able to consult and compare, it seems quite clear that this work has been painted on canvas. This is apparent from multiple horizontal marks that are clearly visible in photographs under raking light, all of which confirm my first-hand impression when I stood in front of the painting in the National Gallery.
>
> The spacing and shape of these marks are compatible with the presence of a loosely woven handmade canvas. The warp is visible horizontally. The thread appears to be irregular but fine, with approximately six threads per centimetre. The weft thread count must also be approximately six threads per centimetre. The weft is less obvious but does appear in certain places. The warp is visible in several details of the painting, always with the same thread count per centimetre, making it impossible to confuse with grain as it appears on a wooden panel.
>
> Moreover, the observed relief cannot be mistaken for marks left by a possible relining canvas[2]:
>
> • the paint layer, where it is thin, appears thinner and more opaque in the indentations than on the relief of the canvas (a characteristic feature of oil painting on canvas).
> • the areas of impasto are not deformed and do not indicate the use of a relining canvas.
>
> A more systematic study and a comparison of photographs of the painting under raking light should provide a more definite answer on the possible presence of an underlying canvas.[3]

The question arises, then, of why both Ludwig Burchard's 1930 authentication report for Van Diemen and Benedict *and* a later one prepared for Christie's in 1980 describe the painting's material as oak panel. The only plausible explanation I could think of was that, whoever had made this painting had, before 1929, stuck

     CANVASSING OPINION

the canvas onto a thin sliver of wood, possibly oak veneer. The wood was then made to look like an even thicker old oak panel by the addition of wooden cross-bars on the back resembling a trellis. Unless it had been taken apart in a workshop, the marouflaged linen could have easily passed for wood.

When I realised that people who knew so much about materials and whose expertise was unquestionable were confirming what I had myself seen, I was delighted. There is such a thing as having a 'feel' for materials. When you work with wood, either as a polisher or as an instrument-maker, you acquire a deep understanding of the idiosyncrasies of each type of wood. In the same way, a restorer of delicate materials like parchment and paper, especially one who has also studied the conservation of Old Master paintings on canvas or on wooden panels, knows and understands better than most people what s/he is seeing. As I have always thought, a good eye is rarer than anyone can imagine. To be able to see flaws, one has to know and to have seen thousands of specimens of painted wood and painted canvas. It takes someone with experience of the material to be able to recognise it.

LETTER TO DR FINALDI

On 11 July 2020, I addressed a letter to the new Director of the National Gallery, Dr Gabriele Finaldi, mentioning, among other things, my findings from the high-resolution photographs and my conclusion that NG6461 is painted on linen. In another one of many coincidences, this was the anniversary of the purchase of the painting by the National Gallery at Christie's in 1980, forty years before!

Dear Dr Finaldi,

As an artist and art historian who worked for many years in London and still visits frequently, may I begin by congratulating you on the reopening of the Gallery? At a time of distress, rancour and economic uncertainty in so many places, the enlightened values which your collection superbly represents are a sorely-needed balm for our souls.

Exactly for that reason, I believe the matters that I would like to draw to your attention are more pressing than ever. As part of your reopening announcement, you singled out some of the Gallery's best-known attractions, including the painting of *Samson and Delilah* which is ascribed to Peter Paul Rubens.

Nobody doubts that Rubens did render that scene, after a commission from the mayor of Antwerp, Nicolaas Rockox, in 1609-10. But the authenticity of the work now in the Gallery was hotly contested after its acquisition in 1980 (as it happens, the acquisition was made 40 years ago today). As your records will show, I led the field among the doubters, along with two fellow students at Wimbledon College of Art. Our research was widely quoted in the press. Our case rested on the newly acquired work's dubious provenance, its physical construction and on significant differences from contemporary copies of the original.

In a number of ways, the case against the authenticity of the Gallery's painting has recently grown stronger, and the matter has become easier to settle, for anyone who approaches it fairly.

In particular, the use of photography to ascertain the precise material composition of a work of art has become much more sophisticated and more widely accessible. There is a simple question about this painting which should now be very easy to answer.

Was this work, as the Gallery asserts, painted directly on wood? Or was it painted on linen canvas stuck onto a thin layer of wood? If the second theory is correct, then the description of the painting in the Gallery's *Technical Bulletin* of 1983, written by the late Dr Joyce Plesters, is invalidated, and all questions about the history of this work are in urgent need of re-examination.

I claim no particular expertise in photography, yet as a member of the public using a mid-range camera I was able to capture some high-resolution images of the painting which strongly support the second hypothesis. I have discussed my images with experienced conservators from several countries and they share that prima-facie assessment.

Apart from this physical evidence, the chain of provenance asserted by the Gallery now looks weaker than ever. The claim of authenticity rests on a certification by Ludwig Burchard who, for all his dedication to Rubens, was far from infallible in his judgement, as has been shown by some diligent research by Kasia Pisarek. The fact that Burchard's brother profited from the work's resale must also taint him as an objective witness.

As your records will show, I was invited in 1996 to watch a dendrochronological test of the painting which, for reasons I can explain in detail, was a spurious exercise. If, as now seems to me very likely, the painting turns out to be on canvas, then the test looks even more dubious than ever.

In good faith, and in a spirit of utmost respect for you and your great institution, I would like to put a question to you. I raise this question openly and I would welcome an open answer.

     CANVASSING OPINION

Is the Gallery now willing to use the latest available methods to re-examine the material composition of this painting, in a way that is transparent and shared with the public, both specialist and non-specialist? Secondly, if the painting is shown to be on canvas, is the Gallery prepared to re-examine its likely pre-history without prejudice?

At the age of 74, I have no interest in burnishing my own reputation or in embarrassing others. Being of Flemish as well as Greek descent, I do however feel an undiminished concern for the integrity of the Rubens legacy, which I truly feel has been tarnished by an unworthy attribution. The Gallery has laboured hard to promote knowledge about Rubens and his magnificent work. I put it to you that this cause could be further advanced by setting the record straight on this sensitive matter.

I have one final reason for persisting. In 1997, a Trustee of the Gallery, a person of great distinction, told me that he believed my doubts were well-founded and that truth would prevail in the end. That Trustee died shortly afterwards but there was a witness to our conversation who confirms what was said. I can provide more details if necessary.

I hope you will understand why I cannot in good conscience let this matter rest.

Yours sincerely, etc[4]

THE REPLY

The Director chose to respond through the Curator of Dutch and Flemish paintings, the scholar Dr Bart Cornelis. His letter amounted to an unequivocal rejection of the doubts about materials raised in my letter, and reaffirmed his conviction about the technical mastery of the work and the greatness of its author.

New York Breakthrough

When I first started trying to solve the mystery of the National Gallery's misattributed acquisition, I never thought that I would find out who had actually painted it. The question "if not Rubens, then who?" was just one of the many questions I kept thinking about. So much time has elapsed, and so little evidence has survived, that looking for the author of a fake painting is a nigh-on impossible quest. Lesser artists have been copying masterworks ever since antiquity.[1] During Rubens's lifetime alone, in the sixteenth and seventeenth centuries, copies of his works were sold by the dozen at the Antwerp Friday Market. We know from his extensive correspondence that Rubens himself found it difficult to control the quasi-illegitimate trade in prints of his work that was taking place under his nose in his hometown, so one can only imagine the exponential growth of copies of his famous works during the centuries that followed.

Everything about the constructed provenance of NG6461 that had been bestowed on it by the Rubenianum scholars and embraced by Christie's (at no expense to themselves) and subsequently by the National Gallery was highly problematic. So where did it come from? What is its real provenance? Clearly, *someone, somewhere, sometime* had painted it.

The *Corpus Rubenianum* states that, after many reappearances over 300 years, the painting emerged again for the last time in Paris in 1929, having been bought there (the *Corpus Rubenianum* omits to say who sold it) by a Dr Benedict of the Van Diemen and Benedict art dealers of Berlin, Germany. This provenance is based on wishful thinking, at best; more accurately, it is a fabrication of hcity-toity nonsense.

In 1983, after it had spent three years in the National Gallery's Conservation Department, the Gallery presented the painting to the world in an exhibition called *Acquisition in Focus*. In the accompanying booklet, Christopher Brown, then Curator-in-Chief and Head of Dutch and Flemish Paintings at the National Gallery, thanks the Rubenianum for allowing him to look at the manuscript notes written by Burchard (the scholar under whose name the *Corpus Rubenianum* is still to this day being published), strictly "under the terms of Ludwig Burchard's will". Earlier, in 1970, in his catalogue of paintings of the Flemish School owned by the National Gallery, Gregory Martin had similarly acknowledged that "the heirs of the late Dr L. Burchard and the authorities of the City of Antwerp" had allowed him "for exceptional reasons" access to the notes when he was researching Rubens for the National Gallery.[2]

My colleagues and I tried repeatedly to access Ludwig Burchard's notes, which were deposited after his death at the Rubenianum in Antwerp. Several attempts over the years, in writing and in person, were greeted with filibustering, bureaucratic obstinacy, and all in all uncooperative and disruptive responses.

We couldn't help but wonder why Ludwig Burchard's notes on paintings by Rubens and van Dyck are hidden away, inaccessible to the wider community of scholars and to the public more generally. How is it possible to have a multi-volume project in progress with the name of its initiator and editor, Ludwig Burchard, attached to it, and then to exclude from these volumes that person's own notes? Why is information being withheld by the Rubenianum, an ostensibly transparent and purportedly impartial academic institution dedicated to the independent study of Rubens's work and to the dissemination of the aforementioned monumentally ambitious literature? And how strange that Burchard—whose intention, ostensibly, was to bring together all present-day knowledge of the work of Rubens—should have expressly made provisions in his will that would prevent that very thing from happening.

In the end, we find ourselves in a highly dubious situation wherein both the seller and the buyer of a painting are given access to these confidential documents, while the British taxpayer, the academic community, and the public at large are kept away from the information—that is, from the only potentially credible provenance of NG6461.

It was not until the year 2000 that I finally saw for myself the relevant notes that had been theretofore out of the public's reach. Michael Daley had submitted a Freedom of Information Act request, and finally managed to get permission to see the material in the NG6461 dossier at the National Gallery archives.

The most critical discovery was a single photocopy of an undated, typewritten sheet in German **[39]**: the authenticity certificate that Burchard had supplied to Van Diemen and Benedict in 1930, before the firm sold the picture to August Neuerberg in Germany.

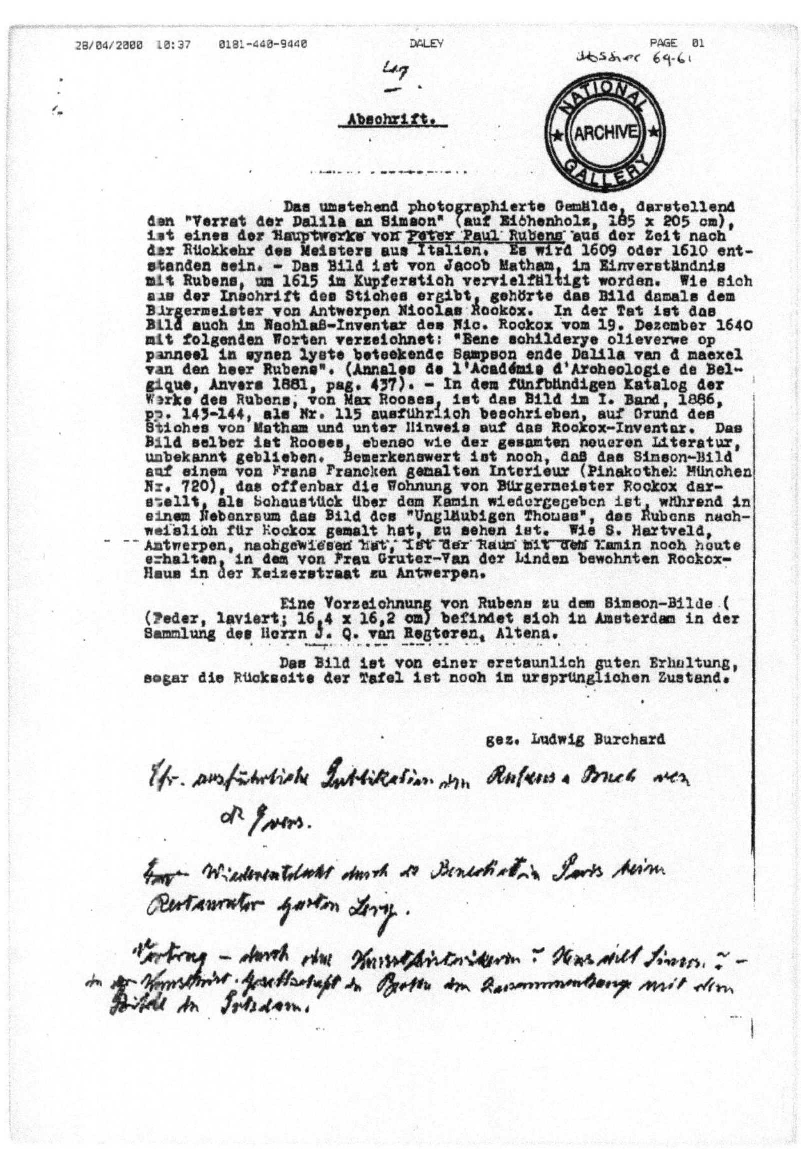

Abschrift.

Das umstehend photographierte Gemälde, darstellend den "Verrat der Dalila an Simson" (auf Eichenholz, 185 x 205 cm), ist eines der Hauptwerke von Peter Paul Rubens aus der Zeit nach der Rückkehr des Meisters aus Italien. Es wird 1609 oder 1610 entstanden sein. — Das Bild ist von Jacob Matham, im Einverständnis mit Rubens, um 1615 im Kupferstich vervielfältigt worden. Wie sich aus der Inschrift des Stiches ergibt, gehörte das Bild damals dem Bürgermeister von Antwerpen Nicolas Rockox. In der Tat ist das Bild auch im Nachlaß-Inventar des Nic. Rockox vom 19. Dezember 1640 mit folgenden Worten verzeichnet: "Eene schilderye olieverwe op panneel in synen lyste beteekende Sampson ende Dalila van d maexel van den heer Rubens". (Annales de l'Académie d'Archeologie de Belgique, Anvers 1881, pag. 437). — In dem fünfbändigen Katalog der Werke des Rubens, von Max Rooses, ist das Bild im I. Band, 1886, pp. 143-144, als Nr. 115 ausführlich beschrieben, auf Grund des Stiches von Matham und unter Hinweis auf das Rockox-Inventar. Das Bild selber ist Rooses, ebenso wie der gesamten neueren Literatur, unbekannt geblieben. Bemerkenswert ist noch, daß das Simson-Bild auf einem von Frans Francken gemalten Interieur (Pinakothek München Nr. 720), das offenbar die Wohnung von Bürgermeister Rockox darstellt, als Schaustück über dem Kamin wiedergegeben ist, während in einem Nebenraum das Bild des "Ungläubigen Thomas", das Rubens nachweislich für Rockox gemalt hat, zu sehen ist. Wie S. Hartveld, Antwerpen, nachgewiesen hat, ist der Raum mit dem Kamin noch heute erhalten, in dem von Frau Gruter-Van der Linden bewohnten Rockox-Haus in der Keizerstraat zu Antwerpen.

Eine Vorzeichnung von Rubens zu dem Simson-Bilde ((Feder, laviert; 16,4 x 16,2 cm) befindet sich in Amsterdam in der Sammlung des Herrn J. Q. van Regteren, Altena.

Das Bild ist von einer erstaunlich guten Erhaltung, sogar die Rückseite der Tafel ist noch im ursprünglichen Zustand.

gez. Ludwig Burchard

39. Authenticity Certificate: From the National Gallery's own archive, obtained through a FOIA request.

The day after we received the certificate, an assistant from the National Gallery telephoned Michael and volunteered the information that the document was dated 1930. However, at the bottom of the paper are three handwritten notes by Burchard himself which must be post-1946, since they contain a reference to *Peter Paul Rubens* by Hand Gerhard Evers, which was not published until 1946. What I surmise must have happened is that Burchard kept a copy of the authenticity certificate he had supplied to the buyer in 1930, and during the following decades added handwritten notes concerning the fate of the painting he had authenticated. I am inclined to believe that these are the notorious 'Notes' on the painting by Burchard which we were not meant to see.

One of the notes reads: "Bought by Dr Benedict in Paris in 1929 from the *conservator* [restorer] Gaston Lévy". At long last we have the only *real* provenance of the painting. These footnotes, scribbled by hand in German, furnish what is by far the most important piece of information contained in the dossier and, for us, a revelation: Gaston Lévy, the man I had been looking for, the man who sold NG6461 to Benedict in Paris in 1929!

GASTON LÉVY

The name Gaston Lévy is as common in Francophone countries as John Smith is in the Anglosphere. A man with a Jewish name that spans continents would be hard to locate. My first port of call was the British Library. To my joy, I found him in a tiny entry in the updated Benezit Dictionary of Artists, which contains biographies of all known painters, sculptors, and engravers from the ancient times to the present day. Gaston Lévy, it turns out, was a Brazilian painter, born in Rio de Janeiro in the nineteenth/twentieth century, who studied at the Real Academia de Bellas Artes de San Fernando in Madrid at the beginning of the twentieth century. It was there that he became part of the circle of Joaquín Sorolla y Bastida (1863–1923), who was later professor of painting there.

VISIT TO MADRID: A COPY BY SOROLLA'S STUDENTS?

I was thrilled to have found a clue to Gaston Lévy's identity—he belonged to the Spanish neo-impressionist school and had studied in Madrid. I immediately decided to visit Madrid and went straight to the Sorolla Museum, a beautiful hacienda-type villa situated in lovely gardens in a quiet neighbourhood in the city.

I was very anxious to see Sorolla's work. The minute I saw the first painting—a picture of some women from Alsace in colourful folk costume—I recognised the style of NG6461! The two paintings shared a neo-impressionist manner, but whereas in Sorolla's late-nineteenth-century work this was not out of place, in our supposed seventeenth-century painting it was.

In Sorolla's large studio there is a huge copy of Velázquez's *Pope Innocent X*, the original of which was later to inspire the painter Francis Bacon in twentieth-century England. This peculiar monochrome copy—which looks like a photograph but isn't—hangs over the fireplace: it is sepia and cream oil paint on canvas, with the background around the Pope's head and shoulders painted black, like a blanket of ink. From afar, it 'worked' as a background, but up close it was very tacky and unconvincing. It established for me that Sorolla and his students, in keeping with the nineteenth-century tradition of art education, had been in the habit of copying Old Masters as an exercise in learning classical techniques. That practice had been introduced at the Real Academia by José de Madrazo as early as 1820.[3]

The Real Academia des Bellas Artes de San Fernando in Madrid is the Spanish equivalent of the Royal Academy in London. It has a museum that houses its collection of Old Masters, until recently hung in a majestic building on the Puerta del Sol. I was fascinated to discover that it held another painting of disputed authorship, occasionally attributed to Rubens: *Susanna and the Elders*.

THE NATIONAL GALLERY'S COMPARISON

The National Gallery, in their repeated press releases defending the attribution of NG6461, have compared it in quality and style with the San Fernando *Susanna and the Elders*. They could not have chosen a painting with a more controversial attribution—one to send more shudders of insecurity down the spines of scholars. *Susanna and the Elders* is not an undisputed original and has serious problems of its own.

It is, admittedly, on the whole and compositionally, a much better picture than NG6461, although it shares with the latter a brashness of colour and execution. It is, conveniently, of a similar scale to NG6461 (198 × 218 cm compared to 185 × 205 cm), and it is placed by certain scholars at the same date as that at which *Samson and Delilah* is meant to have been painted (in 1609–10)—although the National Gallery publications from 1983 onwards reflect an inconsistency of dates. In the *Corpus Rubenianum III / The Old Testament, Susanna and the Elders* is treated as an original by Rubens's own hand, even though several authors in the past believed it was not. Max Rooses, in his monumental *Catalogue raisonné: L'Oeuvre de Peter Paul Rubens* of 1886–92, considered it to have been a workshop painting *only retouched* by Rubens himself. It was bought by the Real Academia de Bellas Artes on 18 January 1778 from the Collection of Prince Pio in Rome and has been there ever since. Only thirty-four years later, in 1812, it was referred to as being the work of Jordaens by Nicolás de la Cruz y Bahamonde. The official catalogue of the museum by E. Torno, from 1929, describes it as being "probably by Rubens" of the Italian period. Closer to the present, it was, significantly, not included in the 1994 exhibition of masterpieces in the museum's collection.

A THEORY STARTS TO SHAPE

Meanwhile, a possible scenario had begun forming in my mind regarding the origins of NG6461. Gaston Lévy, who trained in Madrid during his student years (1901–4), may well have copied—as an exercise, and perhaps even together with other students—well-known paintings as part of his teacher's classes. He probably took upon himself the ambitious task of recreating Rubens's *Samson and Delilah*, then considered to be a lost masterpiece. He would have known of it from Rooses's *Catalogue raisonné*, the 'bible' of all known Rubens works. Lévy may have painted NG6461 in Madrid from the Matham engraving in the *Catalogue raisonné*.

Even more excitingly, Lévy may well have seen the Frans Francken II *Kunstkammer* painting, too. We know that he visited Munich—where the Francken painting was housed in the predecessor of the Alte Pinakothek, on Theresienstraße—in 1909. In fact, we know from his letters to Sorolla, who later became his long-term friend and mentor, that Lévy actually stayed on the same street. Since the exact dimensions of the original *Samson and Delilah* are unknown, he would have had to guess the size. This is not a difficult task if one has seen the Francken interior of Rockox's salon; by comparing it with the known dimensions of people, statues, and other paintings in the room, one can estimate, more or less, how big the original would have been.

I surmise that NG6461 is most probably a legitimate copy that Lévy and his fellow painters (two or three hands are visible) did of a lost Old Master work, the Rockox *Samson and Delilah*, under the supervision of their mentor, Sorolla, in early-twentieth-century Madrid. The missing toes in the composition can now be explained: when students make a copy of an Old Master, it's an unwritten law that they should leave something out, in order not to seem as if they are trying to deceive. The size should differ slightly, as should the composition. In any case, the painting features neo-impressionist brushstrokes, a tell-tale *terminus post quem*.

It is also worth noting that it would have been virtually impossible for a student in the early twentieth century to acquire a huge oak panel, the size of a king-size bed, on which to paint his copy. It would have made far more sense for him to paint on canvas, a much cheaper material that could be rolled up and transported with ease.

GASTON LÉVY IN MADRID AND PARIS

Over the next few years, convinced about my authorship hypothesis, I continued to investigate Gaston Lévy and his life. A young friend helped us with the research. Gaston Infante Lévy was born in Rio de Janeiro in 188? (in the 1900 Madrid census, the last digit is illegible, but it is either '80, '82, or '89). His middle name was also his mother's maiden name. Before the turn of the twentieth century, possibly following the death of his parents in Brazil, he was brought as a child to Madrid, where he lived with his aunt, Maria Infante. After finishing his studies in Madrid, he moved to Paris and set up a conservation studio. He also continued to paint, taking part in various exhibitions and art competitions in the two cities.

In Paris, Gaston Lévy lived at 73 Rue Caulaincourt, the same building where Auguste Renoir, Théophile Alexandre Steinlen, and other artists had their studios. There were also many other famous artists living on the same street, including Henri de Toulouse-Lautrec and Marcel Duchamp. Lévy was also friends with many members of the Spanish community, probably fellow students and acquaintances from his days at the Real Academia.

On discovering that Gaston Lévy had lived in Paris, I visited his haunts near Montmartre. In 2006, I was fortunate enough to be allowed to visit the library of the Museum of the Art and History of Judaism in the Marais, in the beautiful Hôtel de Saint-Aignan. Passing through top security measures, I spent several days looking through the tragic catalogues, handwritten in cursive, of the convoys of all the Jews of Paris who were sent to the concentration camps. Never has calligraphy struck me as more sinister— such tragic fates recorded in such a beautiful way. I felt honoured, moved, and surprised that I was trusted with these rare volumes, that I was allowed to hold them in my hands and turn page after page recording that monumental devastation.

I found thirteen Gaston Lévys in these bloodstained lists. The age and place of birth of each was listed, and I already knew from Benezit that the one I was looking for was born in Rio de Janeiro. None of these Parisian men and boys matched. At the end of the catalogues were three more Gaston Lévys who had no recorded place of birth. I didn't think he was any of them either. I was nonetheless almost certain that he had been a victim of the Shoah. Why does he disappear after 1929?

GASTON LÉVY IN NEW YORK

One evening just before Christmas 2006, sitting at my desk in Paris, I searched online for the name "Gaston Lévy restorer", and the first thing to appear was a photograph with that title. It was a moment I will never forget. My heart leapt. Clicking on the entry, a wonderful black-and-white photograph appeared of a beautifully dressed, well-groomed elderly gentleman who at first glance looked like Gustave Doré, my favourite nineteenth-century illustrator [40]. Sitting in front of an Old Master painting which he had obviously been working on, the man in the photo looked composed, organised, and intelligent. I heaved a deep sigh of relief that Lévy had lived to be an old man.

I immediately looked to see where the photo was from. The Smithsonian Institute had been digitising the collection of the Peter A. Juley & Son fine arts photography firm, who were photographing artists in New York in the 1950s. The photo had only just been digitised. Another two photos from the archive featured Lévy, one of them with two women—probably his wife and daughter—wearing white scrubs and looking as though they were working with him in his workshop.

My excitement peaked. Gaston, who at some point after coming to America had changed the spelling of his name from Lévy to Levi, had escaped the clutches of the Nazis. My mind immediately raced to the Hispanic Society in New York, which his mentor Sorolla had adorned with fourteen monumental paintings.[4]

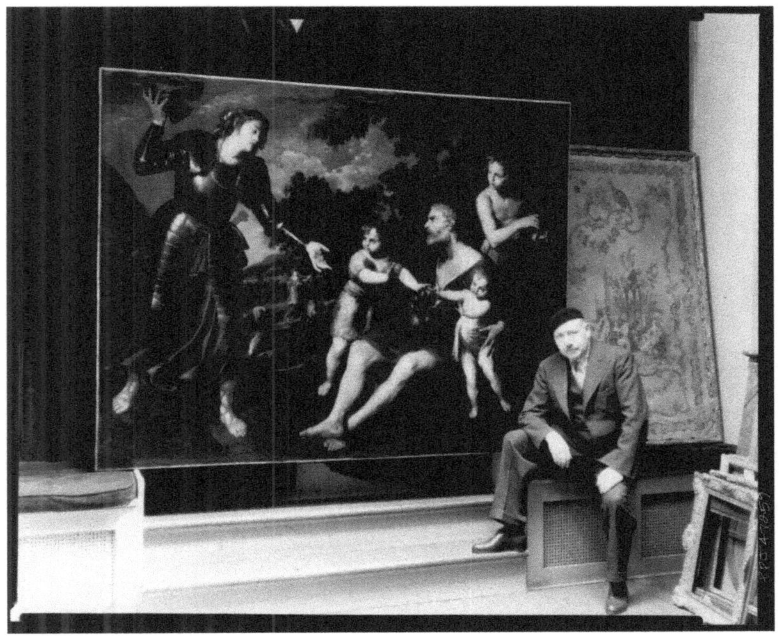

40. Gaston Lévy: Photographed in his studio.

Suddenly I made the connection. The correspondence between Gaston Lévy and Sorolla which I had already discovered confirmed that the two men were very close. Lévy may well have first visited New York with Sorolla in the 1930s, at the time when the latter was doing the paintings.

I phoned my son Nikiforos in London and excitedly told him that I had found a picture of Lévy. Nikiforos responded "OK, now it's easy. You can easily find his obituary online". Manically paying dozens of dollars, I eventually found his obituary in *The New York Times*. Gaston Lévy died in New York in 1957, at eighty years of age. He had been the top restorer at the Frick Collection for many years. Subsequent research showed that Lévy had moved to New York in 1926, taking a studio at 12 East 54th Street. His well-established studio later moved to 16 West 56th Street, and, from what we now know from the Juley & Son photograph, he kept his successful studio until well into the 1950s—although he continued to travel back to Paris, where he retained his prestigious studio in parallel with his New York one.

We do not know the precise circumstances under which the art dealer Benedict bought Gaston Lévy's painting in 1929, but the obvious guess is that it was at Lévy's already well-established conservation studio at Rue La Bruyère. My guess is that although Lévy never would have claimed that his *Samson and Delilah* (NG6461) was a real Rubens, Benedict took the painting to Germany and called in Ludwig Burchard, who in turn authenticated it as a genuine Rubens for the firm of art dealers of which his brother Otto was a partner to eventually sell to August Neuerburg.

I am inclined to venture the following story. The oil painting on canvas (which may have been painted in Madrid by Lévy and his colleagues—or, indeed, only by his colleagues, by his friends from the Sorolla circle of painters—or in Paris, where many of the members of the Sorolla circle had moved to as well as Lévy) was marouflaged by Lévy (an exceedingly competent restorer) on a warped sandwich of cheap woods. Possibly the first layer of the marouflage under the linen was planks of oak veneer. Lévy pasted those thin veneer planks onto pieces of contemporary plywood which altogether formed a slightly warped board which was the size of the painting itself. On the back of this slightly warped wood construction he added a lattice, or trellis, in order to make it look like an antique. Following that, he painted the lattice dark grey—almost black—and then pasted his trademark thin rod of soft, pale-coloured wood around the painting.

He was such a competent and brilliant restorer, and he pasted it so carefully, that he managed to make the linen canvas look as though it was oak—an effect that was also aided by the thin veneer of oak planks sitting just under the surface of the canvas. So artful must his emulation of wood under the paint layer have been that it fooled even experts like Burchard in 1930 and, much later, in 1977, the recipients of the painting when it arrived to be hung for the exhibition of Rubens's work that was held to mark the 400-year anniversary of his birth.

Artificial Intelligence Catches Up

In September 2021, the rapidly advancing science of artificial intelligence (AI) was applied to this art-historical quandary. A Zurich-based duo of high-tech art investigators—both young women with doctorates in mathematical science—at the Art Recognition company used AI to compare brushstrokes in NG6461 with those of scores of confirmed works by Rubens. The result came out overwhelmingly (with a probability of 91.78 per cent) *against* the authenticity of the disputed work.

This cutting-edge research was published in an article by Dalya Alberge in *The Observer* on 26 September 2021 with the title "Was Famed *Samson and Delilah* Really Painted by Rubens? No, says AI" and the headline: "Long-held doubts about the authenticity of the National Gallery's masterpiece, bought for £2.5m in 1980, are backed by pioneering technology".[1]

The National Gallery remained on-message, issuing no formal response until they saw further details of the research. But the verdict gave heart to the growing number of art historians who believe the painting that was bought in 1980 should be re-examined without prejudice, however embarrassing the findings might be.

Three days later, on 29 September, the *Smithsonian Magazine* also ran the story, under the headline "Did Peter Paul Rubens Really Paint 'Samson and Delilah'? A.I. Analysis Renews Doubts Over the Authenticity of a Star Painting in the London National Gallery's Collection". The article stated that:

> After Rockox's death in 1640, the biblical scene vanished from the historical record until 1929, when it—or a copy of it—resurfaced in Paris. Famed German scholar Ludwig Burchard identified the painting as

a genuine Rubens, but vocal critics of the attribution—among them independent scholar Euphrosyne Doxiadis—argue that the work may have disappeared, only to be replaced by a fake, as Edward M. Gómez reported for [Der] *Spiegel* in 2005.[2]

The implications of the story go far beyond a single painting, or indeed a single collection. Everywhere else in the Western world, a new spirit of open enquiry and debate is compelling the owners and keepers of seemingly venerable works of art to submit them to honest investigation. New, unobtrusive instruments for examining the structure and chemical composition of disputed objects, as well as other technological innovations, have been, and are being, developed, especially in the United States. Dutch and German curators are establishing the principle that members of the art-loving public must be kept fully informed, and even welcomed as participants, when contentious works of art are being debated. Great museums like the Rijksmuseum, the Louvre, and the Prado are anxious to tell the world about the powerful equipment they are now using to investigate disputed artefacts.

But the British art establishment, including the bosses of the nation's greatest public gallery, has stayed aloof from this trend. As I have experienced first-hand, any outsider to London's charmed world of experts and pundits can expect to be vilified and marginalised—with lamentable consequences for the state of scholarship at large. The National Gallery and its circle might be forgiven for making a wrong judgement—but it is much harder to forgive suppression of all reasonable debate.

Having battled with this subject for such a long time, I have felt many ups and downs connected to my initial impulse to accuse those who are to blame for this art-historical travesty.

Émile Zola's *J'accuse* in defence of Dreyfus and, indeed, going further back, Demosthenes' *Philippics*, have both been on my mind throughout this long fight for the truth. Initially, as the action of my drama took place in England, and as the original *dramatis personae* were British, I accused the National Gallery of having in its collection a blatantly fake Rubens.

Today, thirty-six years into this battle, I see clearly that the people I should have been accusing from the start were the scholars in Antwerp at the Rubenianum. After all, the National Gallery follows the scholarship of those wise people of the north. Perhaps the National Gallery in 1980, when they put their newly bought prize possession on the backstage operating table of their Conservation Department, became aware of the painting's inadequacies. Perhaps, their state-of-the-art equipment allowed them, over the three years that they kept the painting there, to become acquainted with the true materials of the picture. This we do now know.

I have concluded that the picture is not even painted on wood. Years of scrutiny have convinced me that it is painted on canvas. But who am I to claim that the National Gallery is shamelessly lying to the public, when they say that they agree with the scholars in Belgium that the picture is a seventeenth-century original?

The 'Rubens police', as I refer to them, the scholars 'defending' the artist's legacy, consistently portrayed me as a troublemaker—a title I am, by the way, proud to have earned. Thinking of myself like the "boy who breathed on the glass in the British Museum"[1], I have been made to feel that I was committing a hineous crime, just for daring to question authority and speak publicly about art and about the value of careful observation—areas in which I have been trained since childhood.

Am I arrogantly claiming that the hyping of NG6461 in scholarly books and articles on Rubens was an immediate reaction by the keepers of the painting, the guardians of its claimed paternity, to a trivial and 'uninformed' complaint by three students in 1992? Yes, absolutely. In 2006, in a huge and magnificent exhibition of Rubens's work in Lille, France, the museum bookshop was flooded with monographs on the painter, all of which contained a colour reproduction of the wretched NG6461. Was the National Gallery handing out copyright-free images to every scholar who happily included it? After all, no serious objections to its authenticity had ever been made.

Scholars exercise the courtesy of respecting each other's dictums almost to a fault. The young scholar Joanna Woodall, who wrote to Julius Held about (and thus at least appear to endorse) our objections to the authenticity of the painting back in 1988, speedily made a u-turn when Held wrote back that not only were we—her students at Wimbledon—wrong, but, also, that it was one of his favourite paintings of all Rubens's oeuvre.

Another defender of the National Gallery during the early stages, Professor Edward Hall of Oxford University and a Trustee of the Gallery, wrote to us that we were "barking up the wrong tree" when we suggested that perhaps the panel on which NG6461 was painted was not dendrochonologically old enough to have been painted on in 1609. I was not yet fully convinced, as I am now, that the painting is on linen. I archived his letter and kept it as one more sign of how vigorous, even if not rigorous, the defence of a supposed national treasure can be.

THE RUBENIANUM

Having been caught in a maelstrom of hype created by the National Gallery around the notorious painting in the years following their purchase of it, I was temporarily blind to the fact that the Gallery was only following the general scholarly consensus that this was the original that Rubens painted for Rockox in 1609. The Rubenianum has pronounced in no uncertain terms that Rockox's painting which hung in the Kaiserstraat for thirty years, around the corner from their luxurious offices, is the one now owned by the National Gallery.

In January 2018, I wrote to the head of the Rubenianum, Arnout Balis, requesting to meet him there. He did me the honour of answering my email immediately, telling me that he knew about my objections, and that, since I had initially contacted him through his niece in Brussels, he would gladly see me at his home in that city. I thanked him and said that perhaps we should agree to disagree, and that is what we both decided to do. But the friendly way in which we waved an academic goodbye to each other does not stop me from pronouncing my accusation against the Rubenianum.

Concluding this book, I want to denounce the Rubenianum for having perpetuated an entirely mistaken theory about the quality of NG6461. By inviting the painting to hang, supposedly once again, over the original Renaissance fireplace of the Great Salon in the Rockox House in 2008, they only made the painting look silly and false. Their refurbishing of the Great Salon with intersecting shelves concealed the fact that the painting was far too small for the space and far too small compared to the fireplace below it, making it look even more out of place. Renaissance fireplaces in Flanders were monumentally large and made people standing under them seem dwarfed by their size. One has only to visit the Plantin-Moretus Museum of Printing in Antwerp to see fireplaces of these proportions.

For the few weeks that the exhibition lasted, the National Gallery offered twenty-four-hour protection for their prized possession on a level that would make even Mona Lisa blush. The popular imagination is captivated and manipulated by such overt acts of guardianship.

I accuse the Rubenianum of lacking the courage to go back on Ludwig Burchard's opinion of this picture. I accuse them of not publicising the whole story of how this painting was found and in whose hands. It was presumably Ludwig Burchard who, when the picture was brought to Germany, pontificated that this was the lost *Samson and Delilah* painted for Rockox by Peter Paul Rubens. Gaston Lévy had, I believe, back in Madrid in the early twentieth century, been imaginative and creative in his attempt with his mentor Sorolla to recreate a lost masterpiece. Ironically, in March 2019 the National Gallery held an exhibition of Sorolla's work. I was very tempted to remind them that they have an extra Sorolla in their Rubens collection.

We are tired, in 2024, of fake news and photoshopped images. Does the truth still matter in our day and age? I would like to follow Albert Camus's philosophy and say that, like him, I feel inside me a perpetual sunshine which refuses to be darkened by the too-many shadows cast by the dystopia in which we live. Bertrand Russell felt "unbearable pity for the suffering of mankind". I, too, feel for the suffering of humanity—and God knows we see so many images of it on the internet and in the accelerating news which reaches us. Compared to human lives being lost, what does it matter if a two-by-two metre painting in a museum in London misrepresents a dead artist, no matter how great he may have been? Well, it does matter. It matters because the truth matters. As Isaiah Berlin told me, "The truth will come out in the end, it always does". And we would be deplorable human beings if we didn't do our bit about it.

Acknowledgements

In an age of censorship, fear, and truth-suppression, I am deeply grateful to everyone at ERIS who remained unswerving, supportive, and committed throughout: specifically my publisher, Alex Stavrakas, and my editor, Angus Ledingham—both of whose solidarity, care and visualization made this book a reality.

Special thanks are due to my brilliant fellow painters Siân Hopkinson and Steve C. Harvey, who, having seen the weakness of NG6461 in the National Gallery in 1988, convinced me to fight the fight for the memory of Rubens. They both bravely embarked with me on the initial year of my research to prove to others the correctness of our perception. Had it not been for their insistence and passion for art, as well as for their stunning quality as painters, this book would never have existed. Further heartfelt thanks are also due:

To my son, Niki Mardas, without whose help from the age of thirteen this book would have never materialised. This year my son turned fifty, and he has been consistently supportive of my demanding project. He brought clarity to my research throughout the years and successfully, I believe, tempered down my impassioned style of writing. He is also responsible for building two websites, www.After Rubens.org and www.InRubensName.org.

To my friend the Flemish genealogist Jan Caluwaerts, who delved into the seventeenth-century archives in Antwerp and discovered unpublished documents which supported my suspicions.

To my friends, the late Ruth Rosenberg and Shalom Shotten, who instantly saw the artless brushstrokes of the painting and encouraged me in my project; to the late Ian Sutton, whose brilliance and humour lightened the task of writing this book; and to my dearest friend, Emily Lane, who, together with Ian, painstakingly helped me follow my arguments to their logical conclusions.

To the restorer Georgios Boudalis and the artist Stéphane Treilhou, who shared with me their wisdom on materials.

To the late Jan Bosselaers for his trust in my integrity, and to his son, Mark Bosselaers, who copies Rubens in a really convincing way.

To Marilena Kassimatis and Nedis Dimitrakos for giving me the opportunity to meet Sir Isaiah Berlin.

To *Artwatch* and Michael Daley, director of *Artwatch UK*, who embraced my thesis all those years ago and who, with surgical precision, demolished the totally fabricated, false provenance constructed by various Rubens experts and art historians. Being an artist himself, he saw the flaws in the picture and famously said of them "usually there is a cherry on the cake, but in this case the faults are cherry upon cherry upon cherry". Alongside Michael I must remember with gratitude the late Jim Beck, founder of *Artwatch International*, who also instantly saw the weaknesses of the painting and who invited me to give a seminar to his postgraduate students at Columbia University.

To my 'brother in art' Harold Van de Perre, the Flemish artist who, with his brother, made the excellent films about Peter Paul Rubens for Belgian television. He immediately agreed with my perception of the fake painting and was personally offended by the misrepresentation of "our beloved Rubens".

To the Aegean Centre for the Fine Arts and Jane and John Pack, who have given me the opportunity to give lectures to their students about the 'fake Rubens' over the past twenty-five years. This chance solidified my doubts about the painting's authenticity, because I had to analyze and explain how, and why, it was not genuine, and have my argument withstand scrutiny. To Jane for her acute observations concerning the fatal faults of the copyists of the *Samson and Delilah*, as well as for having taught me the technique of Rubens, who painted with his "precious oil" without ever using solvents—a technique which she worked out by herself.

To friends who understood and added to my thirty-seven-year-long research, namely Rachel Howard, to whom I owe my own amazement with the city when we travelled together to Antwerp. To her unforgettable and magical parents, Dizzy and Charlie Howard. To Rosemary Tzanaki, who brought 'Ph.D.-dom' and love to my project. To Kasia Pisarek for her brilliant Ph.D., "Rubens and

Connoisseurship: On the Problems of Attribution and Rediscovery in British and American Collections (Late Nineteenth-Twentieth Century)". To my friend the Flemish artist Peter Macken, for his help in Antwerp and with all the Flemish documentation about Rubens's work, and to the Irish poet Rory Brennan, who shared his wisdom and his poetry with me.

There are many more friends and colleagues who helped me throughout this research of a lifetime. I could not possibly list them all, but I wish to give special mention to Nikos Anatolitis, Paul Hetherington, Trevor Sather, Ellen Sutton, Vangelis Hatziyiannidis, Clare Maxwell-Hudson, Vassilis Coukis, Terry Gilliam, Alecos Levidis, Ivan Masteropoulos, Mónica Robledo de Pablo, Ruchdi Maalouf, Vassiliki Politi, Anna Stellatou, Kyriakos Anastasiadis, George Menegakis, Konstantina Theodorou, Hylton Philipson, Helen Grove-White, Nigel Haigh, Achilleas Tzallas, Bob Gates and Daphne Becket. To the Flemish artist Alexandra Cool who made Antwerp feel like home again. Finally, boundless thanks are due:

To my dear friend, the author Bruce Clark, whose love and faith in me and in Greece helped me persevere.

To the man in my life, the painter and writer Rafael Sinclair Mahdavi, for his forbearance and love.

To my family and especially my daughter, Emma King, for her constant support, encouragement, and love, and to my daughter-in-law, Nicola Mardas, for her help and love. And, of course, to my four grandchildren, Finn King, Maia, Tatiana, and Andreas Mardas, who make my life a blessing.

To my brother, Apostolos Doxiadis, and my sisters, Anthy and Cali, for believing in me and for their unwavering support.

Lastly, to my late mother, Emma Doxiadis Scheepers, who lived until the age of 100. She repeatedly made me promise that I would drop this project, knowing how dangerous life can be when you insist on telling the truth.

Notes

CHAPTER ONE: SEEDS OF DOUBT

1. Lucy Norton (trans.), Hubert Wellington (ed.), *The Journal of Eugène Delacroix* (London: Phaidon Press, 1951).

2. Peter-Paul Rubens, *The Letters of Peter Paul Rubens*, Ruth Saunders Magurn (ed. and trans.), (Evanston, IL: Northwestern University Press, 1991), 291. Rubens wrote to Pierre Dupuy, the Keeper of the King's Library in Paris, every Thursday between 1626 and 1628.

3. "Arte de la Pintura" by Francisco Pacheco, quoted in Alexander Vergara, *Rubens and his Spanish Patrons* (Cambridge: Cambridge University Press, 1999), 189–91.

4. Ibid.

5. When I visited the Princeton Picture Library in 1997 (a treasure trove before the time of the internet), I had the opportunity to look at seventeenth-century *Samson and Delilah*s by various artists, in small black-and-white photos. I was stunned by the huge number of Flemish and Dutch artists of the time who painted this subject. Rembrandt—slightly younger than Rubens and a great admirer of his work—painted his own enormous *Samson and Delilah*, exhibited in the Vienna and Frankfurt Rubens Exhibition in 2018. One of Rubens's own star students, Anthony van Dyck, painted a *Samson and Delilah*, now in the Dulwich Art Gallery.

6. Malcolm Gladwell, *Blink: The Power of Thinking Without Thinking* (Boston, MA: Little Brown, 2005).

7. Max Friedländer, *From Van Eyck to Brueghel* (London: Phaidon Press, 1956), v.

8. R.-A. d'Hulst (e.a.) *L'Erection de la croix* (Brussels: Editions de Iassa, 1992).

9. In fact, when in Rome, Rubens had copied one of Michelangelo's

Ignudi in the Sistine Chapel. When he ran out of paper, he drew the missing toes under some drapery on another sheet of paper. Likewise, in his drawing of a *Nude Man Kneeling*, the right foot is cropped. Rubens meticulously drew it in its entirety, in a blank area to the left of the footless leg. These two examples serve as important proof that Rubens must have believed these expressive extremities to be vital to the dynamics of the human, and particularly the male, figure. See *ArtWatch UK* newsletter 11, Autumn 2000.

CHAPTER TWO: RUBENS IN ANTWERP

1. Charles Baudelaire, "The Beacons", in Charles Baudelaire, William Aggeler (trans.), *The Flowers of Evil* (Fresno, CA: Academy Library Guild, 1954).

2. Peter-Paul Rubens, *The Letters of Peter Paul Rubens*, Ruth Saunders Magurn (ed. and trans.), (Evanston, IL: Northwestern University Press, 1991).

3. Ibid.

4. Max Rooses and Charles Ruelens, *Correspondance de Rubens et documents épistolaires concernant sa vie et ses œuvres* (Antwerp: J.-E. Buschmann, 1909), 156.

5. Perhaps the simplest refutation of Sperling's assessment comes in a letter Rubens wrote on 12 May 1618 to Sir Dudley Carleton, Ambassador of James I at The Hague: "Your Excellency has taken only the originals, with which I am perfectly satisfied. Yet Your Excellency must not think that the others are mere copies, for they are so well retouched by my hand that they are hardly to be distinguished from originals. Nevertheless, they are rated at a much lower price". (Rubens *Letters*, cit. at Ch. 1, n. 2).

6. According to Arnout Balis, it originated with late seventeenth-century writers—Giovanni Pietro Bellori, Joachim von Sandrart, and Roger de Piles—who were trying to interpret works attributed to the master long after his death, and was 'confirmed' by Sperling.

7. In a letter Rubens wrote in May 1611 to Jacob de Bie, with whom he, Rockox, and a number of humanists had collaborated on the publication of the coin collection of Charles de Croy, Duke of Aarschot.

8. Peter Paul Rubens and Ruth Saunders Magurn, ibid.

CHAPTER THREE: OPENING PANDORA'S BOX

1. Geraldine Norman, "£2.5m Rubens for National Gallery", *The Times*, 12 Jul 1980.

2. Geraldine Norman, "The Unkindest Cut", *The Spectator*, 18 Jul 1980.

3. Judith Judd, "Fury Over Rubens Fee", publication unknown.

4. *Samson and Delilah by Sir Peter Paul Rubens*, auction catalogue (London: Christie's, Manson and Woods Ltd, 1980).

5. Inscription/dedication on bottom right side of inverted engravings (my translation).

6. Erik Duverger, *Antwerpse kunstinventarissen uit de zeventiende eeuw* (Brussels: Paleis der Academiën, 1989), 382–3.

7. Ibid.

8. FelixArchief, Antwerpen (City Archives in Antwerp) Collection: OCMW (Public Assistance), 1782#2507.

9. Ibid.

10. Max Rooses, *Rubens* (Philadelphia, PA: J.B. Lippincott Co. and London: Duckworth and Co., 1904), i: 136–7.

11. Rudolf Oldenbourg and Wilhelm von Bode (ed.), *Peter Paul Rubens* (Munich and Berlin: R. Oldenbourg, 1922), 85.

12. *Samson and Delilah by Sir Peter Paul Rubens*, auction catalogue (London: Christie's, Manson and Woods Ltd, 1980), my translation.

13. Ibid.

14. Ibid.

15. Ibid.

16. Christopher Brown, *Rubens: Samson and Delilah* in *Acquisition in Focus* exhibition booklet (London: The National Gallery, 1983).

17. Hans Gerhard Evers, *Rubens und sein Werk: neue Forschungen* (Brussels: Neue Forschungen, 1944).

18. G. Gepts, R.-A. d'Hulst, F. Baudouin, *P.P. Rubens, Peintures, Esquisses à l'huile, Dessins* (Antwerp: Musée Royal des Beaux-Arts, 1977).

19. Ibid.

CHAPTER FOUR: SAMSON'S MISSING TOES

1. *Samson and Delilah by Sir Peter Paul Rubens*, auction catalogue (London: Christie's, Manson and Woods Ltd, 1980).

2. John Herbert, *Inside Christie's* (London: St Martin's Press, 1990), 126.

3. Ibid. 126.

4. Ibid. 126.

5. Ibid. 128.

6. Arnout Balis, "'Fatto da un mio discepolo': Rubens's Studio Practices Reviewed", in Toshiharu Nakamura (ed.), *Rubens and his Workshop: The Flight of Lot and his Family from Sodom* (Tokyo: The National Museum of Western Art, 1994), 99.

7. Julius Samuel Held, *The Oil Sketches of Peter Paul Rubens: A Critical Catalogue* (Princeton, NJ: Princeton University Press, 1980).

8. Roger d'Hulst and Marc Vandenven, *Corpus Rubenianum Part III* (London: Harvey Miller Publishers, 1989), 114.

9. Joyce Plesters, "'Samson and Delilah': Rubens and the Art and Craft of Painting on Panel" in *National Gallery Technical Bulletin* (London: National Gallery Publications, 1983), 7, 33.

10. Julius Samuel Held, *The Oil Sketches of Peter Paul Rubens: A Critical Catalogue* (Princeton, NJ: Princeton University Press, 1980), 432.

11. Ibid. 432.

12. Ibid. 432.

13. Julius Held to Joanna Woodall, personal correspondence, 13 Jan 1989.

14. Roger d'Hulst and Marc Vandenven, *Corpus Rubenianum Part III* (London: Harvey Miller Publishers, 1989), 113.

15. Roger d'Hulst and Marc Vandenven, *Corpus Rubenianum Part III* (London: Harvey Miller Publishers, 1989), 114.

16. "Faithful Miniature Reproductions", *Oxford Companion to Art* (Oxford: Clarendon Press, 1905), 433: General catalogue, Alte Pinakothek München 1986, 211, "a specialist in the depiction of picture galleries with an accurate reproduction of the paintings contained therein".

17. Rudolf Oldenbourg and Wilhelm von Bode (ed.), *Peter Paul Rubens* (Munich and Berlin: R. Oldenbourg, 1922), 85.

CHAPTER FIVE: DAVID AND GOLIATH

1. Joanna Woodall letter to Julius Held.

2. Ibid.

CHAPTER SIX: BLOOD IS THICKER THAN WATER

1. Arnout Balis, "Antwerp, Foster-Mother of the Arts: Its Contribution to the Artistic Culture of Europe in the Seventeenth Century", in Jan Van Der Stock, *Antwerp: Story of a Metropolis, 16th–17th Century, Antwerp* (Seattle, WA: University of Washington Press, 1993), 115.

2. Conrad Busken Huet, *The Land of Rubens* (Amsterdam: Sampson Low and Co., 1879).

3. Ibid.

4. Paul Huvenne, *The Rubens House Antwerp* (Brussels: Crédit Communal, 1990), 21.

5. Peter-Paul Rubens, *The Letters of Peter Paul Rubens*, Ruth Saunders Magurn (ed. and trans.), (Evanston, IL: Northwestern University Press, 1991).

6. Huvenne (cit. at n. 4), 30.

7. Hans Gerhard Evers, "La Galerie d'Art du Bourgmestre Rockox", *Apollo, Chronique des Beaux-Arts* (Oct 1942), 11.

8. The painter Michael Reynolds (quoted by Dalya Alberge in *The Times* of 19 Jun 1996) saw the hand not of Rubens but of Jacob Jorčaens, and he was supported in that opinion by the *Sunday Times* art critic Waldemar Januszczak.

9. John Rupert Martin, *Rubens: The Antwerp Altarpieces: The Raising of the Cross and The Descent from the Cross*, Norton Critical Studies in Art History (London: Thames and Hudson, 1969).

CHAPTER SEVEN: THE KEEPER OF THE KEYS

1. Christopher Brown, *Flemish Paintings (The National Gallery Schools of Painting)* (London: National Gallery Publications, 1987).

2. Michael Levey, *Director's Choice: Selected Acquisitions 1973–1986* (London: National Gallery Publications, 1986), 19.

3. Colin Wiggins, *Frank Auerbach and the National Gallery: Working after the Masters* (London: National Gallery Publications, 1995).

4. Christopher Brown, *Rubens's Landscapes* (London: National Gallery Publications, 1996).

5. Andrew Graham-Dixon, "The Hair Apparent", *The Independent*, 19 Mar 1991, London.

6. Edward Thomas Hall to Euphrosyne Doxiadis, personal correspondence, 19 Feb 1992.

7. Christopher Brown, Chief Curator National Gallery, to Euphrosyne Doxiadis, personal correspondence, 28 Feb 1992.

8. Geraldine Norman, "£2.5m Rubens for National Gallery", *The Times*, 12 Jul 1980.

9. David Jaffé, "Rubens Back and Front: The Case of the National Gallery 'Samson and Delilah'", *Apollo* (Aug 2000), 21–4.

10. Joyce Plesters, "'Samson and Delilah': Rubens and the Art and Craft of Painting on Panel", *National Gallery Technical Bulletin* (London: National Gallery Publications, 1983), 7, 36.

CHAPTER EIGHT: SAMSON AGONISTES

1. James Beck and Michael Daley, *Art Restoration: The Culture, the Business, and the Scandal* (New York and London: Norton and Company, 1993).

2. Verax: "truth-teller". Pseudonym used by several critics of the establishment from the seventeenth century onwards, most recently Edward Snowden.

3. Quoted in Jaynie Anderson, "The First Cleaning Controversy at the National Gallery, 1846–1853", in *Appearance, Opinion, Change: Evaluating the Look of Paintings* (London: United Kingdom Institute for Conservation, 1990), 3–7; reproduced in David Bomford and Mark Leonard (eds.), *Issues in the Conservation of Paintings*, (Los Angeles, CA: Getty Conservation Institute, 2005), 441–53.

4. Toshiharu Nakamura (ed.), *Rubens and his Workshop:* The Flight of Lot and his Family from Sodom (Tokyo: The National Museum of Western Art, 1994).

5. The Getty Kouros Colloquium, Athens, 25–27 May 1992; published by the J. Paul Getty Museum and the Nicholas P. Goulandris Museum of Cycladic Art, 1993.

6. See <https://www.getty.edu/art/collection/object/103VNP>.

CHAPTER NINE: BLINDED BY SCIENCE

1. Dalya Alberge, "National Gallery Rubens Is Put to The Tree-Ring Test", *The Times*, 19 Mar 1996.

2. Brian Sewell, "It's a Real Rubens, Make no Mistake", *Evening Standard*, 4 Jul 1996.

3. Brian Sewell, "Gems Amid Lunatic Jargon", *Evening Standard*, 4 Dec 1995.

4. Michael Daley, "Is This a Copy?", *Art Review*, Feb 1997; "Is this really a Rubens?", Jul/Aug 1997; "The Back Is Where It's At", Jun 2000. Michael also dedicated two issues of the *ArtWatch UK* Newsletter to the subject: "Who Tampered With This Label?", 11, Autumn 2000, and the "Rubens Special Issue", 21 (Spring 2006).

5. Brian Sewell, "To a Dabbler in the Dark", *Evening Standard*, 2 Jun 2000.

6. Joyce Plesters, "'Samson and Delilah': Rubens and the Art and Craft of Painting on Panel", *National Gallery Technical Bulletin*, 7 (London: National Gallery Publications, 1983), 30.

7. Coralie Mills to Euphrosyne Doxiadis, private correspondence, 22 Oct 1996 on AOC Scotland letterhead.

CHAPTER TEN: THE BENEVOLENT BANKER

1. *Samson en Delila, Een Rubensschilderij Keert Terug*, 16.11.2007–10.02.2008, Rockoxhuis, Antwerp. The artwork was heavily promoted.

CHAPTER TWELVE: THE DICTATORSHIP OF EXPERTS

1. Dalya Alberge, "'Expert Denounces National Gallery's Rubens", *The Times*, 25 Nov 1996.

2. Dalya Alberge, "Wood Expert Casts Doubt on Dating of Masterpiece", *The Times*, 27 Aug 1997.

3. John Harlow and Waldemar Januszczak, "National's £40m Rubens Could Be a 'Fake'"; "Rubens's £40m Painting May Be Work of Pupil", *Sunday Times*, 5 Oct 1997.

4. Kasia Pisarek, "Rubens and Connoisseurship: On the Problems of Attribution and Rediscovery in British and American Collections (Late Nineteenth–Twentieth Century)", unpublished Ph.D. thesis (University of Warsaw, 2009).

5. Simon Schama, *Rembrandt's Eyes* (London: Allen Lane, 1999).

6. Michael Daley to Neil MacGregor, correspondence, 2 Apr 1997

7. Neil MacGregor to Michael Daley correspondence, 4 Apr 1997.

8. Ibid.

9. Ibid.

10. David Jaffé, "Rubens back and front. The Case of the National Gallery Samson and Delilah", *Apollo*, Aug 2000, 21–5.

11. Michael Daley, "The Back Is Where It's At", *Art Review*, Jun 2000.

12. Brian Sewell, "To a Dabbler in the Dark", *The Evening Standard*, 2 Jun 2000, London.

13. *Samson and Delilah by Sir Peter Paul Rubens*, auction catalogue (London: Christie's, Manson and Woods Ltd, 1980).

14. Nicholas Penny, *Frames: National Gallery Pocket Guide* (London: National Gallery London 1997).

CHAPTER THIRTEEN: *THE MASSACRE OF THE INNOCENTS*

1. Maev Kennedy, "Rubens Takes The Credit", *The Guardian*, 1 Mar 2002. Interestingly, the slightly smaller original *Massacre of the Innocents* has been shown for years in the Royal Museum of Fine Arts in Brussels, and its attribution to Rubens had never been challenged before 2002.

2. Sotheby's auction catalogue, *Old Master Paintings Part One*, London, 10 Jul 2022, 18–39.

CHAPTER FIFTEEN: CANVASSING OPINION

1. Georgios Boudalis, letter to Euphrosyne Doxiadis, 31 Aug 2020.

2. 'Lining' is the technique of attaching a new fabric support to the back of a canvas painting. This process can help to safely support the painting if the original canvas has been severely damaged or has grown brittle with age. Source: Royal Museums Greenwich (https://www.rmg.co.uk/stories/topics/what-does-lining-painting-mean). Relining is the repeated action of the above procedure.

3. Stéphane Treilhou, letter to Euphrosyne Doxiadis, 1 Dec 2020.

4. Euphrosyne Doxiadis, letter to Gabriele Finaldi, 11 Jul 2020.

CHAPTER SIXTEEN: NEW YORK BREAKTHROUGH

1. Thomas Hovings, *False Impressions: The Hunt for Big-Time Art Fakes* (New York: Simon and Schuster, 1996).

2. Gregory Martin, *National Gallery Catalogues. The Flemish School ca. 1600–ca. 1900* (London: The National Gallery, 1970).

3. Painting teacher José de Madrazo y Agudo (1781–1859), later appointed director of the Prado in 1838, proposed a new curriculum including "copying original paintings". He argued that copying was a good practice, using the example of the good colorists in the Sala Reservada of the Academia, a collection of nudes by artists including Rubens and Titian. See, Esperanza Navarrete Martínez, *La Academia de Bellas Artes de San Fernando y la pintura en la primera mitad del siglo XIX* (Fundación Universitaria Española 1999), 216–19, 343.

4. *Vision of Spain*, also known as *The Provinces of Spain* (1913–19), a series of fourteen canvases commissioned for the Hispanic Society of America. In 2017, the Prado Museum hosted the exhibition *The Treasures of the Hispanic Society of America*, which included paintings by Sorolla and Zuloaga among other nineteenth- and twentieth-century Spanish painters.

CHAPTER SEVENTEEN: ARTIFICIAL INTELLIGENCE CATCHES UP

1. Dalya Alberge, "Was Famed *Samson and Delilah* Really Painted by Rubens? No, Says AI", *The Guardian*, 26 Sep 2021.

2. Nora McGreevy, "Did Peter Paul Rubens Really Paint 'Samson and Delilah'?", *Smithsonian Magazine*, 29 Sep 2021.

AFTERWORD: J'ACCUSE

1. "Three passions, simple but overwhelmingly strong, have governed my life: the longing for love, the search for knowledge, and unbearable pity for the suffering of mankind" from Bertrand Russell, *The Conquest of Happiness* (London: George Allen and Unwin Ltd, 1930).

Illustration Credits

Every effort has been made to trace copyright holders and obtain their permission for the use of copyright material. The publishers greatly acknowledge the permissions granted to reproduce the images in this book and remain grateful to be notified of any possible omissions and incorporate any such corrections in future editions.

[1]   Peter Paul Rubens, *Samson and Delilah*, c.1609–10, oil on wood, 185 × 205 cm (London, National Gallery) © Wikimedia Commons / Public domain.

[2]   NG6461 phtographed by the author.

[3–4] Peter Paul Rubens, *Samson and Delilah*, (detail), c.1609–10, oil on wood, 185 × 205 cm (London, National Gallery) © Wikimedia Commons / Public domain.

[5]   Frans Francken (II), *Supper at the House of the Burgomaster Rockox*, (detail), c.1630–35, oil on oak panel, 62.3 × 96.5 cm, (Munich, Alte Pinakothek München, Collection: Bavarian State Painting Collections) © Wikimedia Commons / Public domain.

[6]   Peter Paul Rubens, *Samson and Delilah*, (detail), c.1609–10, oil on wood, 185 × 205 cm (London, National Gallery) © Wikimedia Commons / Public domain.

[7, 8] Peter Paul Rubens, *Saint Amand with St. Walburga* and *Saint Eligius and Saint Catherine*, reverse of the side panels of the high altar piece *The Raising of the Cross*, 1610, oil on panel, 460 × 150 cm each (Antwerp, Cathedral of our Lady) © Wikimedia Commons / Public domain.

[9]   Peter Paul Rubens, *Portrait of Susanna Lunden(?) ('Le Chapeau de Paille')*, (detail), c.1622–5, oil on oak, 79 × 54.6 cm (London,

National Gallery) © Wikimedia Commons / Public domain.

[10–2] Peter Paul Rubens, *Samson and Delilah*, (detail), *c*.1609–10, oil on wood, 185 × 205 cm (London, National Gallery) © Wikimedia Commons / Public domain.

[13] NG6461 being auctioned at Christie's on 11 July 1980, author's personal archive.

[14] Inventory drawn at the death of Nicolaas Rockox mentioning *Samson and Delilah*, 1640 (Antwerp) © City archives of Antwerp.

[15] Jacob Matham, *Samson and Delilah*, engraving (mirrored as if it was printed), (New York, The MET Museum, The Elisha Whittelsey Collection, The Elisha Whittelsey Fund) © The MET Museum / Public domain.

[16] Jacob Matham, *Samson and Delilah*, *c*.1613, engraving (mirrored as if it was printed), 38 × 44 cm (Budapest, Szépmvészeti Múzeum and also in London, The British Museum) © Museum of Fine Arts, Budapest.

[17] Frans Francken (II), *Supper at the House of the Burgomaster Rockox*, *c*.1630–35, oil on oak panel, 62.3 × 96.5 cm (Munich, Alte Pinakothek München, Collection: Bavarian State Painting Collections) © Wikimedia Commons / Public domain.

[18–9] Inventories, 1641, (Antwerp) © City Archives of Antwerp.

[20–2] Inventories drawn at the time of the death of Jeremias Wildens, 1653 (Antwerp) © City archives of Antwerp.

[23] Inventory drawn at the time of the death of Guillaume Potteau, 1692 (Antwerp) © City archives of Antwerp.

[24] Peter Paul Rubens, *Samson and Delilah*, *c*.1609, oil sketch (modello), 52.1 × 50.5 cm (Cincinnati, Cincinnati Art Museum, Mr and Mrs Harry S. Leyman Endowment) © Bridgeman Images.

[25] Peter Paul Rubens, *Samson and Delilah*, pen and brown ink, brown wash, brown ink framing lines, 16.3 × 16.1 cm with summary sketches in pen and brown ink on the verso (private collection, previously in the collection of Professor J. Q. van Regteren von Altena).

[26] Frans Francken (II), *Supper at the House of the Burgomaster Rockox* (detail), *c*.1630–5, oil on oak panel, 62.3 × 96.5 cm, (Munich, Alte Pinakothek München, Collection: Bavarian State Painting Collections) © Wikimedia Commons / Public domain.

[27] Peter Paul Rubens, *Samson and Delilah*, *c*.1609–10, oil on wood, 185 × 205 cm (London, National Gallery) © Wikimedia Commons / Public domain.

[28] Rubens's tomb inside Sint-Jacobskerk. Author's own photograph.

[29] Peter Paul Rubens, *The Raising of the Cross*, 1610, oil on panel, central panel 460 × 340 cm, each wing 460 × 150 cm (Antwerp, Cathedral of Our Lady) © Wikimedia Commons / Public domain.

[30] Peter Paul Rubens, *The Descent from the Cross*, 1612–4, oil on panel, 421 × 311 cm (central panel), 421 × 153 cm (wings) (Antwerp, Cathedral of Our Lady) © Wikimedia Commons / Public domain.

[31] Peter Paul Rubens, *Samson and Delilah* (detail), c.1609–10, oil on wood, 185 × 205 cm (London, National Gallery) © Wikimedia Commons / Public domain.

[32–4] Peter Paul Rubens, *The Raising of the Cross* (detail), 1610, oil on panel, central panel 460 × 340 cm, each wing 460 × 150 cm (Antwerp, Cathedral of Our Lady) © Wikimedia Commons / Public domain (left); Peter Paul Rubens, *Samson and Delilah* (detail), c.1609–10, oil on wood, 185 × 205 cm (London, National Gallery) © Wikimedia Commons / Public domain (right).

[35] The author's perspective photo-collage of NG6461 based on a sketch done *in situ* in the Conservation Department of the National Gallery during her visit on 23 September 1996, when she saw the painting off its frame.

[36] Photo given to the author by the late Jan Bosselaers, taken while in Antwerp in 1980 © The Estate of Jan Bosselaers.

[37–8] Peter Paul Rubens, *Samson and Delilah* (detail), c.1609–10, oil on wood, 185 × 205 cm (London, National Gallery) © author's personal archive.

[39] Ludwig Burchard, Authenticity Report, 1930 with later notes, (London), from the dossier of NG6411 at the National Gallery.

[40] Gaston Levi (*sic.*) seated in front of painting [photograph] / (photographed by Peter A. Juley and Son), (Washington, Smithsonian American Art Museum, Smithsonian Institution) © Smithsonian American Art Museum.

Bibliography

Alpers, Sveltana. *The Making of Rubens*. New Haven: Yale University Press, 1995.

Avermaete, Roger. *Rubens and his Times*. London: George Allen and Unwin Ltd, 1968.

Balis, Arnout, Frans Baudouin, Klaus Demus, Nora De Poorter, Hans Devisscher, Dirk de Vos, Wolfgang Prohaska, Karl Schütz, Marc Vandenven, Carl Van de Velde, Paul Verbraeken, and Hans Vlieghe. *Flämische Malerei im Kunsthistorischen Museum Wien*. Zurich: SV International Schweizer Verlagshaus, 1989.

Balis, Arnout. *Corpus Rubenianum Ludwig Burchard, Part XVIII, Landscapes and Hunting Scenes*. London: Harvey Miller Publishers, 1986: II.

——. "'Fatto da un mio discepolo': Rubens's Studio Practices Reviewed", in Toshiharu Nakamura, ed. *Rubens and his Workshop: The Flight of Lot and his Family from Sodom*. Tokyo: The National Museum of Western Art, 1994.

Baumstark, Reinhold. *Peter Paul Rubens: The Decius Mus Cycle*. New York: The Metropolitan Museum of Art, The Collections of the Prince of Liechtenstein, 1985.

Beck, James. *Three Worlds of Michelangelo*. New York: W. W. Norton and Company, 1999.

Beck, James, and Michael Daley. *Art Restoration: The Culture, the Business, and the Scandal*. New York: W. W. Norton and Company, 1993.

Belkin, Kristin Lohse. *Rubens*. London: Phaidon Press, 1998.

Bennett, Anna. *Artbook Rembrandt*. London: Dorling Kindersley, 1999.

Bevers, Holm, Peter Schatborn, and Barbara Welzel. *Rembrandt: The*

Master and his Workshop, Drawings and Etchings. New Haven, London: Yale University Press in association with National Gallery Publications, London, 1991.

Bolton, Linda. *The History and Techniques of the Great Masters: Degas.* London: Tiger Books International, 1988.

Bomford, David, Christopher Brown, and Ashok Roy. *Art in the Making: Rembrandt.* London: National Gallery Publications, 1988.

Bomford, David. *Conservation of paintings.* London: National Gallery Publications,1997.

Boni, Armand. *Antwerpens Roem St. Jacobskerk.* Antwerp: Helikon N.V., 1954.

Braham, Helen. *Rubens: Paintings, Drawings, Prints.* London: The Trustees of the Home House Society for the Courtauld Institute of Art, University of London, 1988.

Brown, Christopher. *Making and Meaning: Rubens's Landscapes.* London: National Gallery Publications, 1996.

Brown, Christopher. *Van Dyck.* Oxford: Phaidon Press, 1982.

Buck, Louisa, and Philip Dodd. *Relative Values (or What's Art Worth?).* London: BBC Books, 1991.

Burmester, Andrea, et al. *Flemish Baroque Painting: Masterpieces of the Alte Pinakothek München.* Munich: Hirmer Verlag, 1996.

Cammaerts, Emile. *Rubens: Painter and Diplomat.* London: Faber and Faber, 1932.

Colin, Peter, trans. and ed. *Peter Paul Rubens Correspondance: I, II, Vie Publique et Intellectuelle.* Paris: Bibliotheque Dionysienne, Les Éditions G. Crès and Cie, 1926.

Constable, William George. *The Painter's Workshop.* London: Oxford University Press, 1954.

Coremans, Paul B. *Van Meegeren's Faked Vermeers and De Hooghs: A Scientific Examination.* London: Cassell and Co., 1949.

Cumming, Robert. *Annotated Art.* London: Dorling Kindersley, 1995.

d' Hulst, Roger Adolf, and Marc Vandenven. *Corpus Rubenianum Ludwig Burchard: Part III, The Old Testament.* London: Harvey Miller Publishers, 1989.

Daley, Michael."Is This a copy?", *Art Review*, February 1997.

——."Is this really a Rubens?", *Art Review*, July-August 1997.

——."The Back is Where is it's at", *Art Review*, June 2000.

Díaz Padrón, Matías. *Museo Del Prado Studia Rubenniana, Dibujos de Rubens en el Museo del Prado.* Madrid: Patronato Nacional de Museos, 1977.

——. *El Siglo de Rubens en le Museo del Prado, Catálogo Razonado de Pintura Flamenca del Siglo XVII, Índices y Bibliografía.*

Barcelona: Prensa Ibérical, 1995: I and II.

Doerner, Max. *The Materials of the Artist*, translated by Eugen Neuhaus. London: Granada Publishing, 1984.

Dubon, David. *Tapestries From the Samuel H Kress Collection at the Philadelphia Museum of Art: 'The History of Constantine the Great' Designed by Paul Rubens and Pietro da Cortona*. Oxford: Phaidon Press for the Samuel H·Kress Foundation, 1964.

Evers, Hans Gerhard. *Peter Paul Rubens*, Antwerp, Uitgeverij de Sikkel, 1946.

Feller, Robert L., ed. *Artist's Pigments: A handbook of their History and Characteristics*, I. Oxford: Oxford University Press for the National Gallery of Art, Washington, 1993.

Gage, John. *Colour and Culture: Practice and Meaning from Antiquity to Abstraction*. London: Thames and Hudson, 1993.

Gettens, Rutherford J., and George L., Stout. *Painting Materials: A Short Encyclopedia* New York: Van Nostrand Company, Inc., 1942.

Goldwater, Robert, and Marco Treves, eds. *Artists on Art from the XIV to the XX Century*. New York: Pantheon Books, 1945.

Goodman, Elise. *Rubens: The Garden of Love as Conversatie à la mode*. Amsterdam, Philiadelphia: John Benjamins Publishing Company, 1992.

Van Guldener, Hermine. *Rijksmuseum Amsterdam*. Ahrbeck/Hannover: Knorr and Hirth, 1967, 1976, 1981.

Hardy, William. *The History and Techniques of the Great Masters: Van Gogh*. London: Tiger Books International, 1988.

——. *The History and Techniques of the Great Masters: Turner.* London: Tiger Books International, 1988.

Härting, Ursula. *Frans Francken der Jüngere 1581–1642: Die Gemälde mit kritischem Oeuvrekatalog*. Düsseldorf: Luca Verlag Freren, 1989.

Hebborn, Eric. *The Art Forger's Handbook*. London: Cassell and Co, 1997.

——. *The updated autobiography: Confessions of a Master Forger.* London: Cassell and Co, 1997.

Held, Julius Samuel. Rubens and his circle, (Princeton: Princeton University Press, 1982).

——. *The Oil Sketches of Peter Paul Rubens I and II*. Princeton: Princeton University Press, 1980.

——. *Rubens: Selected Drawings*. Oxford: Phaidon Press, 1986.

Herbert, John, ed. *Christie's Review of the Season*. Oxford: Phaidon Christie's, 1983.

Huvenne, Paul. *Rubens' Assumption of the Holy Virgin in the Cathedral of Our Lady in Antwerp.* Ghent: Openbaar Kunstbezit in Vlaanderen, 1991.

——. *The Rubens House Antwerp.* Ghent: E. de Cuyper, 1994.

Huyghe, René. *L' art et l' âme.* Paris: Flammarion, 1960.

Jennings, Guy. *The History and Techniques of the Great Masters: Renoir.* London: Tiger Books International, 1988.

Junius, Franciscus. *The Literature of Classical Art.* California: University of California Press, 1991: I and II.

Keating, Tom, Geraldine Norman, and Frank Norman. *The Fake's progress: Tom Keating's story.* London: Hutchinson and Co. Publishers, 1977.

Lassaigne, Jacques. *Flemish Painters: The century of Van Eyck.* Lausanne: Albert Skira Publishing, 1957.

Laureyssens, Willy. *Jacob Jordaens aux Musees royaux des beaux-arts de Belgique,* exhibition catalogue. Brussels, 1993.

Lescourret, Marie-Anne. *Rubens: a Double Life* Chicago: Ivan R. Dee, 1993.

Levey, Michael. *Director's Choice: Selected Acquisitions 1973–1986.* London: National Gallery Press, 1986.

Magurn, Ruth Saunders, ed. and trans. *The Letters of Peter Paul Rubens.* Evanston, Illinois: Northwestern University Press, 1991.

Maréchal, Els, and Leen De Jong. *The Royal Museum in Antwerp.* Ghent: Ludion Press, 1990.

Martin, John Rupert. *Rubens: The Antwerp Altarpieces, The Raising of the Cross and the Descent from the Cross.* London: Thames and Hudson, 1969.

Mayer, Ralph. *The Artist's Handbook of Materials and Techniques.* London: Faber and Faber, 1982.

Michel, Jean François Marie. *Histoire de la Vie de P. P. Rubens, Chevalier and Seigneur de Steen.* Brussells: Æ. De Bell, Marché au Bois, 1771.

Miller, Dwight. *C. Macrantonio Francescini and the Liechtensteins,* Cambridge: Cambridge University Press, 1991.

Morrall, Andrew. The History and Techniques of the Great Masters, Rubens, (London: Tiger Books International, 1988).

——. *The History and Techniques of the Great Masters: Rembrandt.* London: Tiger Books International, 1988.

Muller, Jeffrey M. *Rubens: The Artist as Collector.* Princeton: Princeton University Press, 1989.

National Gallery Illustrated General Catalogue, 1973–1986. London: National Gallery Publications, 1986.

Norton, Lucy. *The Journal of Eugene Delacroix.* London, Phaidon Press: 1951.

Oppenheimer, Paul. *Rubens: A Portrait.* London: Gerald Duckworth and Co. Ltd., 1999.

Perryman, Kevin. *Alte Pinakothek München.* Munich: Editions Lipp, Karl M. Lipp Vorlag, 1986.

Plesters, Joyce. "'Samson and Delilah': Rubens and the art and craft of painting on panel", in *National Gallery Technical Bulletin.* London: National Gallery Publications, 1983: 7.

Prohaska, Wolfgang. *Kunsthistorisches Museum, Vienna: The Paintings.* London: C. H. Beck / Scala Books, 1997.

van Puyvelde, Leo. *Les Esquisses de Rubens.* City: Les Editions Holbein, Bâle, 1940.

——. *The Sketches of Rubens.* London: Kegan Paul, Trench, Trubner and Co LTD, 1947.

Von Ravensburg, Goeller. *Rubens und die Antike, seine Beziehungen zum Classischen Alterthum und seine Darstellungen aus der Classischen Mythologie und Geschichte.* Jena: Hermann Costenoble, 1882.

Regner, Konrad. *Peter Paul Rubens: Altäre für Bayern.* Alte Pinakothek, Munich: Studio Ausstellung, 1990.

van Rijn, Michel. *Hot Art Cold Cash.* London: Little, Brown and Company, 1993.

Roberts-Jones, Phillipe. *Old Masters Royal Fine Arts Museums, Brussels.* Tielt: Lannoo publishers, 1986.

Rosenberg, Adolf. *The Work of Rubens.* New York: Brentano's, 1907.

Roskill, Mark. ed. *The Letters of Vincent van Gogh.* London: Fontana Paperbacks, 1983.

Rowlands, John. *Rubens: Drawings and Sketches.* London: British Museum Publications, 1977.

Roy, Ashok, ed. *National Gallery, Technical Bulettin, Vol. 15.* London: National Gallery Publications, 1994.

——. *Artist's Pigments, A Handbook of heir History and Characteristics II.* Oxford: Oxford University Press for the National Gallery of Art, Washington, 1997.

Schama, Simon. *Rembrandt's Eye.* London: Allen Lane, The Penguin Press, 1999.

Schnackenburg, Bernhard. *Flämische Meister in der Kasseler Gemäldegalerie: Staatliche Kunstsammlungen Kassel.* Melsungen: Verlag Gutenberg, 1989.

Scribner III, Charles. *Rubens.* New York: Harry N. Abrams, Inc. Publishers, 1989.

von Simson, Otto. *P. P. Rubens (1577–1640)*. Mainz: Philipp von Zabern, 1996.

Smets, Irene. *The Cathedral of Our Lady in Antwerp*. Ghent, Ludion Press, 1999.

Stephenson, Jonathan. *The Materials and Techniques of Painting*. London: Thames and Hudson, 1989.

Stevenson, Robert A. M. *Rubens, Paintings and Drawings*. Oxford: Phaidon Press, 1939.

van der Stock, Jan. *Antwerp: Story of a Metropolis, 16th–17th Century*. Ghent: Martial and Snoeck, 1993.

Stout, George L. *The Care of Pictures*. New York: Dover Publications Inc., 1948.

Sutton, Peter C. *The Age of Rubens*. Boston: Museum of Fine Arts, Boston, in association with Ludion Press, Ghent, 1993.

Varshavskaya, Maria, and Xenia Yegorova. *Peter Paul Rubens: The Pride of Life*, Bournemouth: Parkstone/Aurora Publishers, 1995.

Vlieghe, Hans. *Corpus Rubenianum Ludwig Burchard: Part VIII, Saints I*. London, New York: Phaidon Press, 1989.

——. *Corpus Rubenianum Ludwig Burchard: Part XIX Portraits II*. London: Harvey Miller Publishers, 1987.

Voet, Leon. *Antwerp: The Golden Age, The Rise and Glory of the Metropolis in the Sixteenth Century*. Antwerp: Mercatorfonds, 1973.

Watson, Peter. *Sotheby's Inside Story*. London: Bloomsbury Publishing, 1997.

Wazbinski, Zygmunt. *Peter Paul Rubens*. Warsaw: Krajewa Agencja Wydawnicza RSW, "Prasa-ksiazka-Ruch", 1975.

West, Fitzhugh, ed. *Elisabeth. Artist's Pigments, A handbook of their History and Characteristics III*. Oxford: Oxford University Press for National Gallery of Art Washington, 1997.

Wheelock Jr., Arthur K., Susan J. Barnes, and Julius S. Held. *Antony van Dyck*. Oxford: Phaidon Press, 1982.

Wiggins, Colin. *Frank Auerbach and the National Gallery Working after the Masters*, London: National Gallery Publications, 1995.

Wittkower, Rudolf, and Margot Wittkower. *Born Under Saturn: The Character and Conduct of Artists: A Documented History from Antiquity to the French Revolution*. New York: W.W. Norton and Company, 1963.

Wood, Andrew Dick, and Thomas Gray Linn. *Plywoods: Their Development, Manufacture and Application*. Edinburgh and London: W and A. K. Johnston, Limited, 1950.

Author Bio

Euphrosyne Doxiadis is a Greek artist and writer. She was born in Athens and studied art in Salzburg, at the Cranbrook Academy of Art in Michigan, and at the Slade School of Fine Art and the Wimbledon School of Art in London. She is the author of the critically acclaimed *Mysterious Fayum Portraits* (London & New York: Thames and Hudson, 2005).

www.ingramcontent.com/pod-product-compliance
Ingram Content Group UK Ltd.
Pitfield, Milton Keynes, MK11 3LW, UK
UKHW050615100325
455970UK00005B/11